ZIXI/06 LT6/05

THE WAYSIDE GARDENS COLLECTION

The FLOWER GARDEN

The FLOWER GARDEN

A Practical Guide to Planning & Planting

Helen Dillon

John E. Elsley, General Editor for The Wayside Gardens Collection

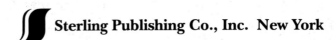 Sterling Publishing Co., Inc. New York

Library of Congress Cataloging-in-Publication Data

Helen Dillon.
 The flower garden : a practical guide to planning & planting /
Helen Dillon.
  p. cm.— (The Wayside Gardens collection)
 Includes index.
 ISBN 0-8069-4291-6
 1. Flower gardening. I. Title. II. Series.
SB405.D55 1995   94–30696
635.9—dc20   CIP

2 4 6 8 10 9 7 5 3 1

First paperback edition published in 2001 by
Sterling Publishing Company, Inc.
387 Park Avenue South, New York, N.Y. 10016

The  Collection Edition

© 1995 by Conran Octopus Limited
The original edition was first published
in Great Britain by Conran Octopus Limited
37 Shelton Street, London WC2H 9HN
Text and original planting schemes © 1994 by Mark Rumary
Design and layout © 1994 by Conran Octopus Limited
Distributed in Canada by Sterling Publishing
C/o Canadian Manda Group, One Atlantic Avenue, Suite 105
Toronto, Ontario, Canada M6K 3E7
Printed and bound in China
All Rights Reserved

American Project Editor	Hannah Reich
Project Editor	Jane O'Shea
Project Art Editor	Ann Burnham
Editors	Carole McGlynn
	Caroline Davison
Designer	Olivia Brooks
Picture Researcher	Jessica Walton
Production	Sonya Sibbons
Illustrators	Fiona Bell Curie
	Vanessa Alford
	Pauline Dean
	Michael Shoebridge

Sterling ISBN 0-8069-0847-5 Trade
0-8069-4291-6 Paper

FRONT JACKET *Ghent azaleas above a carpet of
bluebells.*

BACK JACKET *This herbaceous border includes clumps
of pink* Erigeron, *purple catmint (*Nepeta*) and the
deep purple spikes of* Salvia × superba, *contrasting
with yellow* Anthemis tinctoria *'E.C. Buxton.'*

PAGE 1 *Perennial Oriental poppies (*Papaver
orientale*).*

PAGE 2 *A mixed planting of cornflowers (*Centaurea*),
Dahlia, Cleome and blue Delphinium spires.*

RIGHT *A well-balanced double border in late summer.*

CONTENTS

GARDENING
WITH FLOWERS

Faced with a new garden you can, of course, simply rush off to the garden center in early summer, fill up the car with pots of plants just about to flower, dig little holes wherever there happen to be gaps, push them in and hope for the best. Indeed, there may well be some happy results with this mode of gardening, but a very much deeper level of enjoyment is reached when you start to learn a little about the needs of a plant, to find out what sort of soil and position it prefers, and to cultivate it well so you can see what it is really like—how tall, what color, and exactly when it flowers and for how long. The more you learn about the appearance and behavior of plants, the more magical a garden you can create.

Here we see all the ingredients of a well-planned flower border in high summer with good juxtaposition of height and blend of soft colors. Mixed poppies (including Papaver somniferum) *run through the border, lending an air of informality.* Dianthus *and* Geranium sanguineum *'Album' spill onto the gravel.*

This border of hot colors in the author's garden comprises Heuchera micrantha *'Palace Purple,'* Verbena *'Lawrence Johnston,'* Berberis thunbergii *'Atropurpurea Nana,'* Dahlia *'Bishop of Llandaff'* and Macleaya cordata. *Advice on planting for color is given on pages 58–59.*

There are flower gardens of every size and sort—you can derive the same intense delight by growing some carefully chosen flowers in pots on a city terrace as you will have by modifying and improving a large flower border. The planning is just as meticulous, thinking out color schemes just as much fun, and the anticipation just as exciting, as these two widely different flower gardens reach their apotheoses of color and scent in high summer.

An unforgettable picture comes to mind of a London basement area in which all the romance of the flower garden was captured in a small, dank space, where the sun only reached one corner and then only at midday. There were lilies in profusion, *Lilium regale*, *L. auratum* and *L. longiflorum*, crimson and lime-green tobacco plant (*Nicotiana*) and tall, fragrant *Nicotiana sylvestris*. For structure there was a bay tree (*Laurus nobilis*), *Camellia*, and *Viburnum*. Among the twenty or more different *Clematis* were 'Etoile Violette,' 'Duchess of Albany,' 'Marie Boisselot' and 'Huldine,' climbing and twining their way up the walls, through the area fences, up the steps to the sun above, mingled with white potato vine (*Solanum jasminoides* 'Album'), *Cobaea* with their

RIGHT *A lovely, easy composition using a limited range of plants. Penstemon 'Andenken an Friedrich Hahn' on the right, seen with pink valerian (*Centranthus*) on the left, is propagated from cuttings while the white musk mallow (*Malva moschata alba*), uniting the scheme, is self-seeding. A contrast in texture is provided by woolly *Stachys byzantina.

The author, Helen Dillon, seen in her Dublin garden in the summer.

handsome bell-flowers, various jasmines and a *Buddleia* as an oasis for London butterflies. Long-flowering *Malva* 'Primley Blue' basked in the only sunny spot. Growing in large pots standing in saucers, regularly given liquid feed, unfailingly watered, and their every leaf examined daily for insects, these plants were all in glowing health.

Many lessons were to be learned in that small garden. All the different clematis alone ensured continuity of flower (spring-flowering *C. alpina* and *C. macropetala*, early-summer *C. montana*, and late-summer *C. viticella* cultivars were included), and as there is nothing these beautiful climbing plants like more than to have their roots in the shade and their heads in the sun, they were an ideal choice for the site. The bay tree and *Camellia* provided good evergreen leaves, essential to every flower garden, the tobacco plants were chosen because they are one of the few bedding plants that do well in shade, not to mention their heavenly evening scent.

On a journey round a flower garden, from the largest to the small, there should be an occasional flurry of excitement, a moment of intoxication, and this was offered by the lilies, with their large and lovely flowers and their heady fragrance. On more practical matters, an exceptionally high standard of maintenance was kept up, vital on such an unprepossessing site, since aphids breed at an astonishing rate in city gardens.

The more challenging your site, the more finely tuned your critical eye for a plant will be, and the more discerning your judgment. Does a plant truly warrant the space it is taking? Is it so delightful when in flower that you are prepared to forgive its unseemly late-summer appearance? Does it deserve the extra attention required to grow it well? Constant reassessment of your garden and its plants is the essence of good gardening, and apart from questioning the value of a certain plant, you might also try a little self-criticism as to where you have positioned it. For no matter how many good plants you accumulate, unless they are placed where they will grow well, display themselves to perfection and at

This delightful arrangement could be copied in the smallest garden. Clematis 'Marie Boisselot' winds its way upward while delphiniums, foxgloves, and columbines (Aquilegia) rise from a haze of silver-leaved, shrubby Artemisia. Leave one or two foxgloves to seed for the next year.

the same time enhance their neighbors, all their charm will be lost. This book should help you to focus on suitable plants for *your* garden from the bewildering array in cultivation today.

Good planning, good planting and proper care (all given a chapter to themselves in this book) are the most important elements in making a flower garden, and the guidelines given here should set you thinking along the right lines. After that you are on your own and you will discover which plants you can take liberties with, as well as many suggestions as to how or where to plant something. But do remember that these are only ideas—your most exciting and inventive plans will probably suggest themselves as you go along.

Gardening with flowers, despite attendant headaches, dashed hopes, hard work and setbacks of weather, pest or mysterious disease, is redeemed by many joyous moments as you progress from the first hesitant plantings. You will discover a fresh way of looking at the world, a worm's-eye view reserved only for serious weeders, like the way little rivulets of water run down the center of a *Hosta*, straight to the roots—a good example of the brilliance of design you will notice countless times in the world of plants. The flowers themselves, in their infinite diversity, each with its own singular beauty, have such a talent to enthrall that once you start making a flower garden you may find yourself caught in a magical spider's web from which you never wish to escape.

RIGHT *In this inviting garden all the plants will give a grand show in early summer for many years, with no attention whatsoever (except the delphiniums). Lime-green, fluffy-flowered* Alchemilla mollis *and* Geranium × magnificum, *with violet-blue flowers in the middle of the picture, are useful accompaniments to your mid-summer border, equally happy in sun or shade.* Campanula glomerata *(bottom left) will run about, but to keep it in full vigor, divide and replant it every few years.*

PLANNING
THE FLOWER GARDEN

Whether you are starting from scratch or reworking an existing garden, there will be problems to overcome as well as satisfaction to be gained in creating your own flower garden. Your starting point may be an expanse of bare soil, a joyous, overgrown muddle of brambles or a rather pleasant mature garden, with a scattering of roses, an elderly lilac and the remains of a rock garden in the middle of the lawn. Whatever your starting point, and whatever type of garden you ultimately wish to create, good planning is needed at the outset.

The simple structure of this garden—the brick path, an inviting seat and enclosing hedges, all the elements of good planning—combine with flower beds in an understated color scheme of pale yellows and creams. The large clump of green-and-white foliage to the left is the beautiful but very invasive variegated ground elder Aegopodium podagraria 'Variegatum.' Contrast of height is provided by fennel (Foeniculum vulgare), Achillea, foxgloves (Digitalis) and Iris.

Working with what you have

Helleborus orientalis
Ballard's strain
Mrs. Helen Ballard,
at her nursery in
Worcestershire, England,
started breeding hellebores
in the 1960s, resulting in
some remarkable cultivars.
The flower colors range
from bluish-black through
to good, clear yellow, as
well as wonderful forms of
the more usual reddish
purple, pink and white.
Woodland plants, best
sited in semi-shade,
hellebores are easy to grow
and tolerant of a wide
range of soil conditions,
provided a generous
amount of organic matter
is worked into each
planting hole, with a
sprinkling of bonemeal.
Their lovely flowers are
better seen if the old leaves
are cut away in mid-
winter (this also helps to
prevent the spread of
fungus diseases).

The perfect site for a garden may only exist in the eye of the mind: imagine a gentle sunny slope, the soil well drained and at the same time rich in humus, as easy to work in the depths of winter as it is moisture-retentive in summer, a soil that is neutral, neither acid nor alkaline, and therefore suitable and adaptable for any plant you might care to grow. Add a patch of light woodland with a stream for shade and water lovers, some sheltering walls for tender shrubs, several mature hedges of yew (*Taxus baccata*) and box (*Buxus sempervirens*) and, of course, a mild climate where it only rains when you want it to and then only at night. Needless to say, the owner of this small paradise would have a deep pocket, endless time and boundless energy for hard work.

Reality is usually quite different from this gardener's paradise. You may have to contend with unsightly views of neighboring buildings that you can do little about, overshadowing trees that rob your garden of light and your soil of nutrients, intrusive pylons or washing lines, or visiting cats. You may have a demanding job or family of small children that leave no time for wandering dreamily around the garden wondering what to plant where, let alone the strength to do some serious digging.

If you have just moved, you may have considered only the suitability of the house itself, its size and number of rooms, and failed to notice that the main garden received little sun and the soil was limy and poorly drained in some areas. If it is a new house, the builder may have irretrievably mixed the topsoil with the subsoil, or perhaps decorated the subsoil with a thin dressing of topsoil, thus lulling you into a false sense of security.

Instead of the scorched-earth look of the patch attached to a newly built house, at the other extreme you may have to hack your way through a jungle of weeds, ideas flooding into your head as you unearth the remains of former paths and discover plants that need rescuing. An inherited garden that has been cared for can pose problems of a different kind. It may all seem pretty to begin with, but strangely unsatisfying. The plants do not quite complement each other and the layout seems a little awry.

However, always remember that one of the curious facts of gardening is that all gardeners think that their garden alone is beset with insurmountable problems—if it is not subject to late frosts, vine weevils and swirling wind tunnels you may be sure they will complain that their soil is sticky, unworkable clay with an abnormally high slug population or alternatively a hot, dry rubble in which even such plants as the Algerian iris (*Iris unguicularis*), notoriously fond of dry conditions, is short of water.

Whether you are starting a garden from scratch, or wanting to beautify an existing one, the first thing to decide is what sort of flower garden you want. Would you like to be able to find something lovely in flower any day of the year or do you want one glorious display of summer color? Perhaps you have fallen in love with lilies, sweet peas, roses or auriculas and want to specialize in growing them. Do you want to set aside an area for growing flowers for cutting, or should they be mixed into the borders (see page 43)? Have you considered making flower beds in particular color schemes? Is fragrance a priority? You may well have all of these requirements, in some measure, but first let us assess the limitations of your existing garden, and consider how we are going to work these ideas in.

The size of the garden

The size of the garden imposes its own set of rules, for the smaller the garden the more each plant must warrant the space it takes up. The first instinct of the new garden owner is to go straight to a garden center and buy a little bit of this and that. Before doing this, consider the remark brilliantly put by Gertrude Jekyll in *Home and Garden*, published in 1900, "Often when I have to do with other people's gardens they have said: 'I have bought a quantity of shrubs and plants; show me where to place them'; to which I can only answer: 'That is not the way in which I can help you; show me your spaces and I will tell you what plants to get for them.'"

Plants in their pots at a nursery all look equally desirable. Before making a purchase, it is important to find out all you can about them. You can of course look them up in books to try and find out their ultimate height and spread. But it may be less easy to discover how long they take to reach their final size, and books may not explain exactly how the plant behaves: does a tree cast a light shade (such as a *Gleditsia*, *Laburnum* or *Amelanchier*), under which it is possible to grow quite a range of plants, or will the soil underneath it become so densely shaded that little else will grow there? (See pages 18–19 for shade-tolerant plants.) Think carefully about this if you want to pack in as many plants as possible.

Another important point to consider when choosing a small tree is to find out how greedy it is. Does it have roots that run about on the surface of the soil, taking all the moisture and plant foods, as a silver birch does? Or can you plant almost up to the base of the tree, as you can with an apple or pear tree? How does a tree or shrub look in high summer when the garden will probably be used most often? The late-summer foliage of shrubs like lilac (*Syringa*), *Philadelphus* and *Forsythia* is a dull, leaden green and no great asset to the garden at that time. Visit other gardens, to learn about what plants look like at maturity and what their contribution is at different seasons.

A neglected and overgrown garden can pose as many challenges as a bare new site. Weed seeds have colonized all empty patches of earth in this garden, and the shrubs and climbers, left unpruned, are straggly in their growth. Although the foxgloves, Lysimachia and Lychnis continue to flower, they will have starved the soil of nutrients.

The climate and aspect

The vagaries of the local climate and the orientation of your garden are two of the most important considerations at the planning stage.

Climate

Both the general climate of your area and the various microclimates within the garden must be taken into account, for even a tiny garden will have its warm corner, its drafty wall and an area devoid of sun.

When you are told that a plant is tender, you imagine this means that the first hard frost will kill it. But it is not as simple as that. Plants can be tender in many different ways. With some, yes, it is the first hard frost that blackens *Dahlia* foliage, South African *Gazania* and *Osteospermum*, tender *Helichrysum* and *Salvia*. But sometimes it is not so much winter cold that kills plants, but lack of summer sun to ripen the wood and give it resistance to cold. And some foolish plants, used to winters where the weather stays cold and there are no false springs, are deceived by a sunny week. They come into leaf too soon and are promptly shriveled by frost. Other plants, alpines in particular, are cold-hardy but sensitive to winter damp, and must be covered with glass or polyethylene.

Cold air flows downhill, just like water. If it becomes trapped by running into a hollow, or by meeting an obstacle such as a high wall, it will form a frost pocket. It is only by working in your garden and observing your plants closely that you find out which are the choice, sheltered spots, and which areas should be reserved for the hardiest customers.

Rainfall is often unpredictable and even in wetter areas there may be drought conditions for part of the summer. So when planting your garden try to keep those plants that will really suffer from lack of water in the same place, the nearer the tap the better, so if water is very short you can easily rescue your astilbes, willow gentians (*Gentiana asclepiadea*), rodgersias, Himalayan blue poppies (*Meconopsis*) and so on.

*Hellebores (*Helleborus orientalis*), snowdrops (*Galanthus nivalis*) and the foliage of* Arum *are suitable spring plants for a shady, north-facing border. The hellebores and snowdrops are decorative for at least three months, and both will self-seed to increase the colony.*

Aspect

The aspect of the garden is a primary consideration. One side of the house will get little light in the darker months, and flowers that have good winter foliage should be the priority here (*Bergenia*, *Epimedium*, *Arum italicum italicum*, *Tellima*, *Brunnera*, *Iris foetidissima*, *Campanula latiloba*, *Helleborus* and *Pulmonaria*, for example). If the entrance to the house is on the sunless side, you could make winter your theme here and plant the essential shrubs of winter, *Jasminum nudiflorum*, *Viburnum farreri* and one of the lovely winter-flowering mahonias (*Mahonia* × *media* 'Charity' or 'Lionel Fortescue').

Wind can damage plants in several ways—by breaking the branches of trees and shrubs, by rocking tall plants and breaking their roots so that they can no longer take up sufficient moisture. Winds also increase the rate of transpiration—too much moisture is lost from the leaves and the plant becomes stressed. A solid structure such as a wall can cause violent turbulence to leeward but a hedge, picket fence or a shelter belt of wind-resistant plants allows the wind to flow through. In windy areas young plants can be protected by screens of fine plastic mesh supported by canes or posts. Town gardens often have the problem of swirling winds that rush along the narrow gap between houses; if you stand in the garden when the wind is blowing hard you will see which are the most protected spots.

The sunny side of the house presents problems of a nicer kind: you have to decide, from a wonderful range of sun-loving plants, which are truly worthy of the premier spot. Make sure that you really love the plants you choose, and are certain that they will grow only here and nowhere else in the garden. You do not want to waste a precious position on something that will do just as well elsewhere.

Shady borders

The meaning of the word "shade," when considered in terms of gardening, can be very misleading. Some of the choicest woodland plants we grow like shade, but the kind of shade they require has to be qualified. Imagine a bed filled with loose, woodsy soil, rich in humus, nicely moist at all times of the year but not too wet, in shade but not overhung by

dense foliage. A tall tree canopy shelters this bed from hot sun and although it is always in shade, there is also plenty of diffused light. No drying wind disturbs the composure of the plants or shrivels their leaves; each autumn a natural mulch of fallen leaves nourishes the soil. This is the bed for *Glaucidium palmatum*, Canadian bloodroot (*Sanguinaria canadensis*), *Jeffersonia*, *Trillium*, *Arisaema*, *Anemonella*, some hardy orchids (*Dactylorhiza*, *Epipactis*) and other beautiful plants for shade.

The other extreme is the condition known as dry shade, in which the soil is robbed of moisture by an underground network of tree roots. If you could X-ray the soil and see the multitude of fine roots, spreading in all directions, rapaciously gobbling up all water and plant foods, you might well hesitate to plant anything! Overhanging trees and high buildings may aggravate the situation by deflecting rain. In a way this part of the garden would be easier to plant, since the range of suitable plants for such a site is relatively limited.

Bearded irises, Stachys byzantina, Lychnis coronaria *and catmint (*Nepeta*) all insist on sunshine, but the peonies (at the top left) will also do in part-shade. Purple-leaved* Cotinus coggygria *is a useful background foliage shrub in sun or shade.*

A bed in dry shade

Many of the plants that do well in shade have good foliage but modest flowers and this is one of the reasons they look appropriate in a diffuse, shaded light; vivid colors belong in the sunshine.

Euphorbia robbiae, in the middle of the plan, has wonderful foliage throughout the year; cut off the old flower stems in late summer. The variegated privet looks very pretty, like a small tree, if you prune off the lower branches close to the trunk.

   Euonymus 'Emerald 'n' Gold,' *Valeriana phu* 'Aurea' and the variegated *Tolmiea* (on the right of the plan) will make a lovely splash of yellow. (Bright, golden ferny-leaved *Tanacetum parthenium* 'Aureum' is planted beside *Valeriana* as the latter goes green in the summer.) If you plant yellow and cream-variegated foliage together they are inclined to detract from each other, so these plants are kept well away from the cream variegation of the privet, *Ligustrum ovalifolium* 'Argenteum,' *Brunnera macrophylla* 'Hadspen Cream,' *Geranium macrorrhizum* 'Variegatum' and *Iris foetidissima* 'Variegata.'

   The three groups of white-flowered Japanese anemones (*Anemone × hybrida* 'Honorine Jobert'), for early autumn, all have a patch of honesty (*Lunaria annua*) nearby to flower in spring. After flowering, pull out the honesty to give the anemone more room, leaving one or two plants for seed. The recommended hosta, *Hosta lancifolia*, is more tolerant than most of dry conditions. Here it is interplanted with *Arum italicum italicum*. As the hosta retires below ground for the year, up comes the arum, to brighten winter with its shining green, marbled leaves.

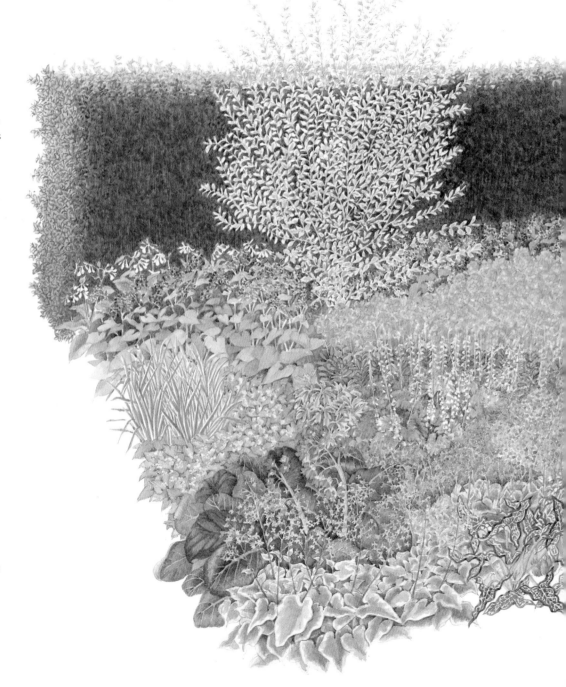

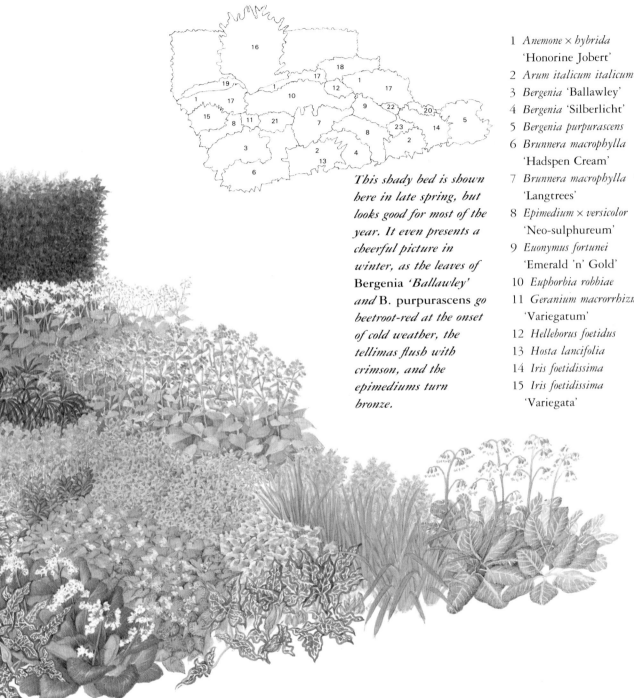

1 *Anemone × hybrida* 'Honorine Jobert'
2 *Arum italicum italicum*
3 *Bergenia* 'Ballawley'
4 *Bergenia* 'Silberlicht'
5 *Bergenia purpurascens*
6 *Brunnera macrophylla* 'Hadspen Cream'
7 *Brunnera macrophylla* 'Langtrees'
8 *Epimedium × versicolor* 'Neo-sulphureum'
9 *Euonymus fortunei* 'Emerald 'n' Gold'
10 *Euphorbia robbiae*
11 *Geranium macrorrhizum* 'Variegatum'
12 *Helleborus foetidus*
13 *Hosta lancifolia*
14 *Iris foetidissima*
15 *Iris foetidissima* 'Variegata'

16 *Ligustrum ovalifolium* 'Argenteum'
17 *Lunaria annua*
18 *Lunaria rediviva*
19 *Symphytum ibericum*
20 *Tanacetum parthenium* 'Aureum'
21 *Tellima grandiflora* 'Purpurea'
22 *Tolmiea menziesii* 'Taff's Gold'
23 *Valeriana phu* 'Aurea'

Other plants that would enjoy this site include:

Acanthus mollis or *A. spinosus* 'Lady Moore'
Alchemilla mollis
Cyclamen hederifolium
Daphne laureola
Dryopteris filix-mas
Galanthus nivalis
Geranium endressii
Geranium phaeum
Hypericum androsaemum
Polygonatum × hybridum
Polygonatum verticillatum
Sarcococca humilis
Sarcococca ruscifolia
Saxifraga × urbium
Tiarella cordifolia
Vinca minor alba
Viola labradorica purpurea

This shady bed is shown here in late spring, but looks good for most of the year. It even presents a cheerful picture in winter, as the leaves of **Bergenia 'Ballawley'** *and* B. purpurascens *go beetroot-red at the onset of cold weather, the tellimas flush with crimson, and the epimediums turn bronze.*

Understanding your soil

Ultimately, the soil is the main dictator of your choice of plants. Although it is possible to create whatever soil conditions you fancy by making up special composts to suit particular plants, it is very much better to work with, rather than against, your existing soil. Happy plants, which enjoy your soil conditions, should make up the most part of the garden. However, some plants are worth every effort to accommodate, either by planting them in a specially prepared bed, or, if they are slightly tender, by trying them out in different parts of the garden. Most gardeners are true speculators at heart, and there is nothing more tempting than an unsuitable plant, either because it prefers, or hates, lime or because it is generally acknowledged to be too delicate for the local climate.

If you are unsure what type of soil you have, take a look around neighboring gardens and see what is doing well—in lime-free areas you will see *Rhododendron*, *Pieris* and other acid-loving plants. If they are not in evidence and you want to grow them, you can always plant them in a container filled with an acidic compost.

A fertile, well-tilled soil is all-important. Even if it means waiting to plant the garden, it is short-sighted to rush preparation of the soil. Nothing you do to the surface of a bed at a later stage, with

Laying a soakaway

Having dug a hole 3 ft. square, line the sides with a fabric filter (geotextile), available from hardware stores. Fill the hole with coarse rubble, such as bricks and large stones, to three-quarters of its depth. Bring the excess fabric around to cover the rubble, then top off the rest of the hole with soil. This soakaway may be sufficient on its own, or it could become the outlet for land drains taking the water away from a damp part of the garden. Land drains come in long, continuous lengths.

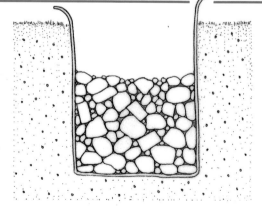

The geotextile acts as a filter to prevent silt filling in the gaps between the stones and stopping the free flow of water.

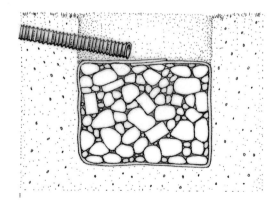

Modern land drains, made of corrugated plastic, are flexible enough to go around a bend on the site.

feeding and mulching, can replace initial thorough digging with liberal additions of manure or compost (see page 81).

Good drainage

How well drained is your soil? Few plants will stand soggy conditions around their roots. Without enough air in the soil, plant roots may rot and the soil organisms essential to healthy growth do not survive. Good cultivation of the soil by deep digging will break up the layer of compacted soil below the topsoil and lavish additions of bulky organic matter

will also help. If you are concerned about the drainage, dig a hole and see how quickly the water runs away. If it has not gone by the following day, you may manage to rectify matters by digging a soakaway (see opposite); this basically consists of a lined, square hole, filled to three-quarters of its depth with rubble. If the situation is more serious, you will have to take advice on laying a series of land drains, leading to a large soakaway or ditch.

If part of the garden is poorly drained and boggy, but stays moist throughout the year and does not dry out in summer, try plants from the list on the right.

PLANTS FOR POORLY DRAINED SOIL THAT IS MOIST ALL YEAR ROUND

Astilbe

Caltha palustris

Chelone obliqua

Darmera peltata

Houttuynia cordata 'Flore Pleno'

Iris ensata (lime-free soil)

Iris laevigata

Iris pseudacorus 'Variegata'

Ligularia dentata 'Desdemona'

Ligularia przewalskii 'The Rocket'

Lysichiton americanus

Lysimachia nummularia

Lysimachia punctata

Lythrum salicaria

Mimulus guttatus

Myosotis scorpioides

Primula florindae

Primula japonica

Primula pulverulenta

Rodgersia

Trollius europaeus

LEFT *Only attempt to grow* Ghent azaleas *(seen here with a carpet of bluebells) if you garden on lime-free soil.*

RIGHT *The large, soft leaves of* Hydrangea aspera *will languish if short of water, while the* Acanthus mollis *would be equally content in a hot, dry place.*

Existing features

Ranunculus constantinopolitanus 'Plenus'

Perhaps due to a number of name changes, this very fine buttercup is not a widely known plant. A herbaceous perennial good for bridging the gap between spring and summer, its flowers are large pompons of tightly packed, glossy yellow petals with bright green centers. The deeply cleft and toothed leaves have patches of pale gray-green that become less pronounced as the year progresses.

Next to weigh up are the existing features of your garden, which, good or bad, you cannot change. Have a look out of the windows of the main rooms of the house and stand in the garden at the major viewpoints. You might get a better idea if you took some photographs, for whereas the eye will conveniently filter out what it does not want to see, the camera is not so easily fooled and will soon spot a pylon or aerial in the distance that you will want to screen from view.

There may be a pretty outlook that you want to include in the overall picture of your garden, like a good tree next door, and you should draw attention to it in the planting plan. But there may equally well be some ugly feature that will have to be disguised with plants. The instant solution would appear to be a coniferous hedge of fast-growing leyland cypress (× *Cupressocyparis leylandii*), but this is rarely a good solution for two reasons. First, from a design point of view, it is far more effective to plant a tree near the house, in the foreground, that will draw the eye and screen the distance. This was brought home to me in a garden in New York, enclosed on all sides by skyscrapers: groups of silver birches had been planted near the house and their white stems, tracery of branches and delicate foliage both attracted the eye and veiled the hard lines of the surrounding buildings. Second, more applicable to the smaller garden, by the time the hedge reaches a suitable height, it will have starved the area of plant foods, moisture and light.

Deciding which plants to keep

"Existing features," in the garden sense, usually includes plants. More than likely you will already have inherited plants of every sort, from mature trees and shrubs to herbaceous plants and bulbs. If you have just moved and suspect there may be good bulbs you will have to wait until spring to see what comes up. If it is a long-established garden, there may be some good old cultivars of herbaceous plants that will need to be propagated and looked after.

Cast the cold eye of discrimination over the existing trees and shrubs. If the garden is neglected there may be some fine specimens that just need rescuing from the undergrowth. If there are any misshapen conifers, take them out, since they are never going to improve. Old yews and hollies will stand hard pruning to shape and are worth preserving as they are slow to grow. Lilacs, berberis and many other shrubs can be cut almost to the ground and will start again. If you are wondering whether to take out a tree or shrub, bear in mind that it will cause less upheaval to take it out to begin with than to disturb the garden when it is established.

Camouflaging a garden shed

This practical but quite commonplace shed has been turned into an attractive garden feature. Flagstones lead to the door where a pair of ball-shaped box (*Buxus*) mark the entrance. *Viburnum davidii* and *Skimmia* in the surrounding bed make the shed seem more part of the garden. *Akebia quinata* is climbing over the shed, masking it with quiet green foliage. In late spring its chocolate-purple flowers will appear and, after a hot summer, you may be surprised by the sight of a few extraordinary, large violet-gray fruits.

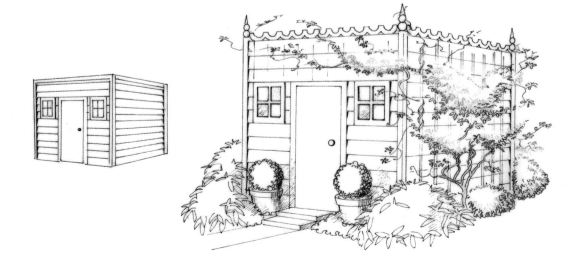

*A garden shed, nicely integrated with the garden. A climbing hop (*Humulus lupulus*) is starting to wind its way up the trellis, while annual pink cosmos, purple and pink clary (*Salvia sclarea*), fuchsias and penstemons make a happy, informal mass of flowers. To camouflage a shed in a shady part of the garden, you might choose* Clematis montana *or a honeysuckle.*

The working area

If you want to grow plants well, you will need a place for the compost heap, farmyard manure, topsoil, leaf mold, sand and grit. And you must have somewhere to keep the tools and the lawnmower. It may be a good idea to tuck all this away at the end of the garden, but think carefully before you do this. Do make sure that it is really easy to get at, so you never skimp on adding a little bit of extra goodness to your soil. Also, when it comes to tidying up in autumn and there are huge amounts of vegetable matter to transport to the compost heap, you do not want it to be too far from your center of operations. But if you are short of space, do not let your working area occupy any valuable planting areas.

Camouflage

Sometimes the more you try to disguise some ugly, permanent feature in the garden, the more you seem to draw attention to it. In *The Education of a Gardener*, Russell Page (perhaps the most eminent garden designer of this century) remarks, "Wobbly planting tries to camouflage yet only accentuates what it is meant to hide." Thus, it is often better to pretend that an ugly old shed was the very thing you always wanted, and to turn it into an attractive feature in itself. The one shown in the illustration (left) has had decorative wooden gingerbread, with a finial in each corner, attached to the roof. It has then been painted dark green, the best color for merging into the background. Planting around the feature gives it a proper setting in the garden.

23

The time factor

Dwarf bearded irises have much less obtrusive fading leaves in late summer than the taller sorts, and will still give a good show with less regular division, provided they are planted in full sun.

The choice of flowers you are going to grow greatly depends on how much time you will be able to give to the garden. If you have not got time to grow a plant well and give it all the extra attention it needs —for example, to stake your delphiniums, prune your large-flowered roses and cluster-flowered roses, feed your clematis, support your sweet peas, bed out your annuals, split up your primulas from time to time, not to mention dividing your bearded irises every few years—you can simply grow alternative plants instead.

Choosing the plants

There is a wonderful diversity of easy plants that need no staking, can take considerable drought, will go for years without division, require no regular feeding and are not particular as to soil or position. You can concentrate on making a good garden out of these plants alone if your time is limited. There is nothing that really compares with the vivid blue spires of large-flowered hybrid delphiniums, but they must be immaculately staked, fed and watered to give of their best. Rather than suffer the reproach of seeing their lovely flowerheads bespattered in mud, or lolling from broken stems, gardeners with only a few hours to spare on the garden might replace them with one of the monkshoods, such as *Aconitum* 'Bressingham Spire,' 'Newry Blue,' or *A. × cammarum* 'Bicolor,' a charmer in blue and white. If you still crave brilliant delphinium blue, try larkspurs or one of the smaller species, such as *Delphinium tatsiense*, that grows to only 2 ft., does not need staking and seeds itself freely.

Many of the old roses and nearly all rose species do not insist on pruning and will forgive you by blooming just the same if you neglect to feed them, provided they are given a good start in life. And instead of the large-flowered clematis that demands a rich diet, try some of the species like *Clematis alpina* or *C. macropetala* that do not need pruning and survive on leaner conditions.

If you are prepared to forego the heavenly scent of annual sweet peas because you have too little time to erect proper supports, grow *Lathyrus latifolius*, the perennial pea, in its beautiful white form 'White Pearl'; it can be trained through a shrub, rambling through the flower border, or tumbling down a bank, so that you can forget about staking. With no time for bedding out annuals, grow only those that seed themselves without your remembering to do it for them (see page 53). And you can avoid the fussier primulas that need constant division by growing vigorous species like *Primula florindae* (tolerant of ordinary border conditions although considered a water-lover) with its scented, lemon-yellow flowers dusted with farina, or some easy Candelabra primula such as *P. japonica*. These will look after themselves by seeding around, so even if vine weevils attack the parent plant there are always young plants coming on. If you love bearded irises, the dwarf sorts will go on flowering without regular division for longer than their taller cousins.

A lawn is unequaled for providing a sheet of plain green to offset colorful flower beds but there is no doubt that it is time-consuming. However good the borders are looking, if the lawn is unkempt the whole effect will be spoilt. In a small garden you could use paving and plenty of box in pots or in the ground (or both) to ease the eye.

Money is a further consideration. If this is in short supply, you may have to grow many plants from seed or from cuttings acquired from friends. In fact, a shortage of money can make you a better gardener for you have to learn more about the craft. Join the specialist plant societies, and study their seed lists: they are full of rare and desirable plants for you to try. You will have to start off with small plants and you should spend any extra money you have on getting your soil right. Do not skimp on loads of manure, topsoil, leaf mold and bags of general fertilizer and bonemeal.

Age and time scales

Age is something to be thought about on many levels when planning the garden. If you are young and intending to move house soon, you will not want to wait many years for a tree like the dove or handker-chief tree (*Davidia involucrata*) to produce its white bracts. Instead you will want to plant shrubs that mature and flower quickly (see the list on page 32), and which are easy to root from cuttings, so you can take young plants with you when you move. Old plants of box move very well, and you can steal a march on time for your next garden by taking them with you. Yew trees up to 6½ ft. tall will move if well watered for the first year; although they take

some time to get going again, you will be able to start off with a decent-sized specimen. Roses, even if the plants are old, move well if they are cut back hard and any damaged roots trimmed. And there is no excuse not to collect any herbaceous plants you like, as they will enjoy the move to new ground.

Regarding age at the other end of the scale, the true gardener is always thinking of next spring, and many octogenarians are still growing lilies from seed, with little thought of the years they take to come into bloom.

Staking is essential for tall herbaceous plants such as these delphiniums. Rosa 'Rambling Rector' will climb to 20 ft. but will need tying back against the wall at intervals.

Achieving your own style

RIGHT *The garden has all the ingredients of a formal design, including rectangular box (*Buxus sempervirens*) beds with restrained planting of standard 'Iceberg' roses and pyramidal yews, enclosed by a yew hedge in the background. Ground-cover plants to the right include Pachysandra.*

Although very informal in style, there are underlying structural elements to this garden. The wooden dividing fence and the grass path that leads the eye to the focal point of the stone seat give form to exuberant planting of Stachys byzantina, lavender, a double Argyranthemum (formerly Chrysanthemum), fennel and fruit trees.

You will have at the back of your mind throughout the planning stage a picture of the style of flower garden you would like, and you need to translate this into what are its essential components.

Decide first of all whether a formal or an informal style would best suit your house and its setting. To simplify the difference between the two styles, the formal is designed on straight lines, with geometric shapes of squares, rectangles or circles with a strict pattern of clipped yew and box, and the informal on more natural lines with gentle curves, meandering paths, and a mass of flowers spilling over the edges.

The subject of curves requires some comment. If you look at a mountain path worn by sheep, or a long-used footpath through woodland, you will see there is always a reason for a bend or curve, whether it is to circumvent a large rock, a tree or a stream. Even in a garden, people want to go from A to B by the most direct route, and the path to the compost heap or parsley patch should be as straightforward as possible. All too often you see gardens with little wiggly paths, put there for no particular reason. If you want a curve, let it make a definite statement by giving it generous proportions, and plant a large shrub, such as *Mahonia*, at its widest point.

Even William Robinson, who believed Nature herself should be the only true model for garden design, said in *The English Flower Garden*: "A straight line is often the most beautiful that can be used; but its use by no means implies that we are not to group our plants or bushes naturally alongside it."

A strong, definite structure will help to pull all the elements of your garden together. Some of the most successful gardens rely on a very formal layout, using straight lines for the paths, lawns and flower beds, and allow the effect to be softened and mellowed by plants. These will soon make spreading mats of foliage, spilling over the straight lines, forming comfortable bulges, propping themselves up on the hedges, climbing and sprawling into one another, and forming a lovely informal tangle. By keeping the man-made parts of the garden—the

lines of path, lawn or hedge—strictly formal and letting an enthusiasm of plants have its way, you can create a delightful cottage garden effect. Alternate the sizes of the groups of plants by planting some large patches, some small and the odd singleton, and then let self-seeding plants—foxgloves, campanulas, cowslips, poppies, *Viola tricolor* and so on—pop up here and there, making the whole thing into a glorious muddle, but still within the confines of a strong framework. This unpretentious cottage garden style is complete when you mix some vegetables with the flowers. Large, wavy-edged blue-gray leaves of sea kale (*Crambe maritima*) look marvelous in the border, bright green parsley is most effective in making gray plants seem all the more silver, and red-leaved frilly lettuces can enhance a color scheme in the garden as well as in the salad bowl. Add some apple and pear trees (very good for the small garden as they do not rob the surrounding soil) and wild strawberries that will seed about in part-shade.

If you want to try out a style that is not specially in keeping with your home, make it in a secluded place tucked away behind high hedges or walls. Several of the best-known gardens in England, such as Sissinghurst and Hidcote, are gardens of compartments, surrounded by formal hedges, forming outdoor "rooms." By enclosing a piece of ground in such a way, you make a stage on which flights of gardening fancy may take place, different moods are created, and you may pretend for a moment that you are in Italy or else taken back in time to sixteenth-century England. In these hidden little gardens the outer world is far away and imagination can take over. Surprising as it may seem, this is just as applicable to small gardens. By dividing them with a simple trellis or hedge, you create an air of mystery, which invites you to go and find out what lies beyond.

The most important thing to keep in mind is that this is *your* garden. Each garden is unique. You must never be intimidated by any book or person about what style you choose, how you design it, or your choice of plants for it—it is your own personal essay in dealing with a particular plot of land.

A sunny wall

The warmest, most protected part of your garden will probably be a sunny wall. When planting against a wall, try to strike a happy balance of shrubs that make satisfying bulges (like the *Bupleurum*, *Itea* and *Carpenteria*) and delicate, twining climbers (like the *Clematis* and *Solanum*).

The flower bed at the foot of the wall, well drained by the searching roots of the shrubs, is the perfect position for some special bulbs such as *Nerine undulata* and *Amaryllis belladonna*. *Iris unguicularis* shelters under fragrant winter-flowering *Daphne bholua*.

The gray foliage of *Convolvulus cneorum*, *Lavandula × intermedia* 'Hidcote Giant,' *Lavandula lanata* and the lovely lacy silver of *Senecio vira-vira* (formerly *S. leucostachys*) add continuity, as does the repetition of *Gypsophila* 'Rosenschleier'; trim this after the first flowers fade to have more flowers into the autumn. *Lavandula* 'Hidcote Giant' goes on and on flowering.

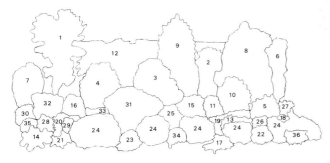

Many of the plants on this list are tender and should be replaced with hardier species if you garden in a cold climate.

On the wall
1 *Azara microphylla* 'Variegata'
2 *Buddleia crispa*
3 *Bupleurum fruticosum*
4 *Carpenteria californica*
5 *Ceratostigma willmottianum*
6 *Clematis texensis* 'Etoile Rose'
7 *Daphne bholua*
8 *Itea ilicifolia*
9 *Pittosporum tenuifolium* 'Silver Queen'
10 *Rosa × odorata* 'Mutabilis'
11 *Senecio vira-vira*
12 *Solanum jasminoides* 'Album'

Flower bed at base of the wall
13 *Arum creticum*
14 *Bergenia ciliata*
15 *Cistus* 'Silver Pink'
16 *Convolvulus cneorum*
17 *Convolvulus sabatius*
18 *Cyclamen coum*
19 *Epilobium canum* 'Dublin'
20 *Erodium pelargoniiflorum*
21 *Euphorbia myrsinites*

22 *Geranium renardii*
23 *Geranium traversii elegans*
24 *Gypsophila* 'Rosenschleier'
25 *× Halimiocistus wintonensis* 'Merrist Wood Cream'
26 *Helianthemum* 'Beech Park Red'
27 *Helleborus × sternii* 'Boughton Beauty'
28 *Iris* 'Cherry Garden'

29 *Iris* 'Green Spot'
30 *Iris unguicularis*
31 *Lavandula × intermedia* 'Hidcote Giant'
32 *Lavandula lanata*
33 *Nerine undulata*
34 *Origanum* 'Kent Beauty'
35 *Origanum rotundifolium*
36 *Yucca filamentosa* 'Variegata'

The following plants would also enjoy this warm spot:
Abelia × grandiflora
Artemisia 'Powis Castle'
Ceanothus 'Puget Blue'
Choisya ternata
Cistus laurifolius
Clematis armandii
Calamintha nepeta
Cestrum parqui
Coronilla glauca
Clianthus puniceus

Cytisus battandieri
Daphne × burkwoodii 'Somerset'
Erysimum 'Bowles' Mauve'
Gladiolus 'The Bride'
Hebe
Luma apiculata 'Glanleam Gold'
Perovskia 'Blue Spire'
Romneya coulteri
Salvia microphylla var. *neurepia*
Wisteria sinensis

The planting against the wall and in the flower bed at its base is seen in late summer, when most of the climbers, shrubs and herbaceous plants chosen for this favored spot are in full flower.

Making a plan

The importance of planning a flower garden in stages, in terms of time and expense, should be emphasized. Always remember that running a garden is rather like running a business: defining the priorities comes first.

When making a garden it is much better to start off at the beginning rather than in the middle. Of course you can just let the garden gradually grow, and as your taste changes, knowledge of plants expands and visual perception develops, you start making adjustments. You alter the shape of the lawn, add a new path or two, decide you have too few, or too many, evergreens, extend or reduce the paving area, simplify the planting, in some areas add a focal point, or decide that you have put one in the wrong place and move it. New plants are bought without thought and scattered here and there. You think that the garden needs more height and plant another tree, or perhaps it needs less shade, so another tree comes out; plants are constantly being disturbed by being moved to where you imagine they are going to grow, or look, better. But this haphazard approach is, ultimately, time-wasting and unsatisfactory. In the long run, much time and money will be saved by planning the garden in stages, and carefully finishing one at a time.

Clearing the weeds

If the garden is heavily infested with serious weeds (bindweed, quack grass and ground elder), the very first necessity is thoroughly and meticulously to clean the whole area—weeds such as these think nothing of a layer of cement or paving stones over their heads and will quickly make their way up the sides or through the cracks. The safest way is to clear the ground by digging and picking the weeds out by hand, but this is time-consuming and you have to make sure that bits of root are not overlooked. You must also be extra careful not to propagate pernicious weeds by accident—a small portion of chopped bindweed root will behave just like a root cutting and start to grow immediately in the freshly dug soil. You could spray a weed-infested area with an appropriate herbicide, but beware of damaging any plants you wish to keep (see page 81).

Try to resist the temptation to start buying plants until the soil is totally clean of weeds: if you have ever spent half an hour trying to disentangle quack grass (a master of disguise) from the roots of some plant, you would understand why. Use annuals for the first year if you do not have time to clear the ground properly (see page 73).

Enhancing paved areas

There are many ways to make a path or area of paving a more integrated, and therefore more sympathetic, element of the garden. Several ideas are given on the right.

If you have to use concrete slabs for paths and paving, interspersing them with bricks or gravel laid in patterns such as those shown on the far right, will help to mellow the harsh look of new concrete. Allowing plants to spill onto the edges of concrete-paved areas, or to grow between paved units, will further soften their appearance.

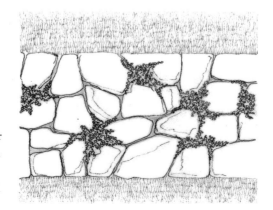

Irregular paving can be enhanced by leaving gaps in between for plants.

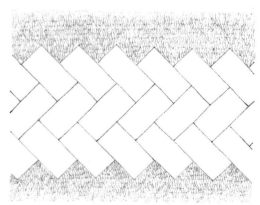

Brick can be laid in a variety of interesting patterns; herringbone (shown here) is one.

Laying paved areas

Having dealt with any serious weeds, you can start to think about laying down the hard landscaping—the paved areas such as paths, terraces and patios. This is probably the largest initial expense in creating a flower garden. Building materials suitable to your area should be chosen for paths as well as steps and walls to keep a unified appearance, wherever possible. But if you have to use concrete slabs, try to soften their look (see below). The new paths will immediately give you access to all parts of the garden, whatever the weather, dry-shod and with a wheelbarrow.

You need to give some serious thought to where you will have a sunny, sheltered, paved area, for sitting in the sun, for entertaining and for children to play. Ideally it should be immediately outside the house, but if the main garden faces east or west you may well need two areas—one to catch the morning and one the evening sun. If the most sunny, sheltered area of the garden is away from the house, make sure there is easy access to the terrace by a good path. Whatever you do, make sure the terraced area is large enough—you will want plenty of space for pots of flowers to soften the effect of the paving slabs.

The use of rounded pebbles or gravel softens the straight lines of concrete slabs.

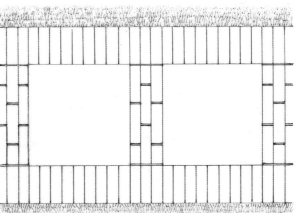

Bricks can be incorporated if the spacing is worked out.

It will help to mellow the harsh look of concrete slabs if you intersperse them with small sections of brick or irregular paving (right). The author's garden is seen here, with her border of hot colors in the background. In the foreground bed the underplanting of hostas and lobelias beneath Cornus controversa *'Variegata' is echoed by blue* Convolvulus sabatius.

The flower beds

**QUICK-GROWING
SHRUBBY PLANTS TO
FILL A YOUNG GARDEN**

Abutilon vitifolium

Artemisia 'Powis Castle'

Brachyglottis laxifolia

Cistus

*Euphorbia characias
    wulfenii*

Fuchsia

Lavandula

Lavatera

Penstemon

Rosmarinus

When deciding where to position the flower beds, an important point to realize is that it is far more difficult to make a successful bed if it is seen in its entirety with one glance (that is, if it is parallel to the house or the main viewing point). If there are any gaps, they will be immediately noticed, and you will have to be much more skillful about arranging shapes and colors. However, if the flower bed is seen end-on (in other words, if it is at right angles to the house or main viewing point) it holds some mystery simply because it is not seen all at once. And if some important plant has gone out of flower, or some of your color-scheme has gone awry, you are more likely to get away with it.

One of the most common mistakes is to make the beds too small. It is hard to achieve a good effect with plants in a very narrow bed, but with a good depth from front to back you can create a much more interesting balance of plant color and form. Ideally, a herbaceous border should be at least 10 ft. in width. Always prepare your flower beds thoroughly (see page 81) before planting them. If your paved area is near your warmest wall, make sure you leave room for a good-sized bed here to experiment with the more tender plants.

Try to avoid meaningless wiggles (see page 26) in the shape of your beds and think in terms of wide, gracious curves or generous, rectangular beds. Avoid any shape reminiscent of innards—kidney-shaped beds have no place in the garden.

The lawn

After digging the flower beds comes the sodding, or sowing of the lawn if you are having one. Decide at this point whether you would like to have a mowing edge, since it is much less of an upheaval to install it now rather than later. This can be a paved edging, about 1 ft. or a little more in width and sunk about ½ in. below the level of the lawn, which is invaluable as the plants growing on the edge of the flower bed can then fall forward, breaking the formal line of the bed, spreading their leaves and displaying their flowers on sun-warmed stone, rather than flopping onto the lawn and damaging it.

The living structure

The next stage consists of deciding where to place the "living structure" of the garden, the hedges and important trees and shrubs. The balance between the amount of evergreens to deciduous specimens should

Shaping the beds and borders

If you find it hard to visualize the shape of a new flower bed, or want to alter an existing one, try laying out the garden hose (or a row of bricks or stones in a line) into a possible shape. Then stand back and look at it from a distance. Live with it for a day or two before making a final decision.

If you wish to increase the depth of an existing flower border, but without letting it dominate a small garden, consider an outline with generous curves.

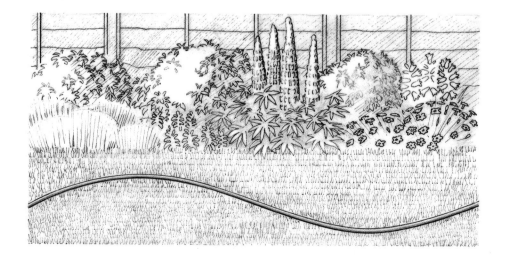

A mowing edge to the lawn, separating it from the beds by a narrow strip of paving or gravel, gives great scope to your design: the strong, straight line of a border can be softened by the planting, but without damaging the grass. The "living structure" of background shrubs and a yew hedge beyond enclose this colorful herbaceous border.

be considered carefully. Too few evergreens can present a bleak appearance in winter, when the eye most craves the pure dark green of yew, box and holly, while too many can give a heavy feeling to your summer borders. You can often tell a garden that has been planted in winter when, to give it an instant, well-furnished appearance, you may see a mass of evergreen plants, predominantly conifers, fresh out of their containers. But how dull such a garden will seem next year, when there is little room for roses, delphiniums and peonies and all the joys of midsummer.

Trees and shrubs for the flower garden could be placed in two categories: those that are planted in prime positions and allowed all the space they need to develop into beautiful specimens, any surround-

ing plants that interfere with their development at a later stage being removed. Such specimen trees and shrubs include a *Magnolia* or a *Cornus*. The other category is those that look quite in keeping mingled with herbaceous plants and annuals in the flower border, like *Weigela* 'Praecox Variegata,' *Genista aetnensis*, *Bupleurum fruticosum*, *Caryopteris*, *Phygelius*, *Philadelphus*, *Cotinus coggygria*, as well as *Hydrangea*, *Buddleia* and shrub roses.

When these first plants go in, the garden can still look very empty. As well as perennials and annuals to fill up this spare ground, you could plant shrubs that grow fast and are easy to propagate so you do not feel guilty when you have to take them out in a few years' time. Great care should be taken about the placing of your important trees and shrubs.

Introducing flowers into the garden

There are many ways in which flowers can play their key role in the garden, and several places in which they can be planted, in addition to the obvious flower beds.

Beds and borders

The mixed border, for all the favorite summer flowers—roses, perennials and summer bedding plants—should always be sited in your sunniest spot. Most gardens will have an equivalent shady bed on the other side, which will give you a chance to exercise imagination and do some research as to what plants would do well in such conditions. The plants you use for this bed depends very much on what type of shade it is (see page 17). And there is no reason why this bed should be any less visually stimulating than a sunny bed. Indeed, some of the most beautiful plants we can grow are shade-lovers, such as *Kirengeshoma palmata* and *K. koreana*, *Meconopsis*, *Smilacina racemosa*, toad lilies (*Tricyrtis*) and *Helleborus*.

Raised beds

Some plants, either too small to survive the rough and tumble of the mixed border, or so special that they warrant close inspection, are better accommodated in a raised bed made of local stone or old bricks (see below). On well-drained soils this needs to be raised no more than about 1 ft., on heavier soils perhaps 2 ft. Particularly if your site is totally flat, giving it height here and there with raised beds immediately adds an interesting new element to the design. At the same time it opens the door to a whole new range of plants, for which you will suddenly have the right spot—wild plants from the mountains of the world, alpine plants, for which the prerequisite is impeccable drainage, as well as all the sun and light going (see also page 76, for a planting plan for a sunny raised bed).

If the retaining walls of your raised bed are built of dry stone, you will be able to grow plants in the cracks between the stones, to tumble down the sides. Raised beds can also be made out of bricks or railroad ties. The bed should be positioned in full sun, well away from the drip of trees.

Some alpines (usually those from high altitudes) require an even grittier, well-drained compost than that described below. If your garden soil is heavy, the bed for these plants should be prepared to a depth of 2 ft., using a mixture of two parts sharp grit, one of soil and one of leaf mold.

Making a raised bed

Unless your soil is very well drained, you will need to fill the bottom third with coarse rubble, such as large stones, with gravel in between. Cover this layer with inverted sods to prevent the next layer trickling through and blocking the drainage. Fill up the bed with a planting mix of two parts of sharp sand or grit, three of good soil, and one of leaf mold. After planting, dress the surface with a 2 in. layer of gravel to keep down weeds, protect alpines from winter damp and to conserve moisture in summer.

A raised bed can be any shape or size but should be positioned in full sun.

A well-drained raised bed in sun is an ideal spot for a collection of alpines, including bright magenta-flowered shrubby Penstemon, *yellow* Sisyrinchium macrocarpon *and spiky silver-leaved* Celmisia semi-cordata 'David Shackleton' *to the left.* Ramonda myconi *grows in more shade at the base of the wall. The eye-catching striped leaves of* Iris pallida 'Argentea Variegata' *remain fresh until autumn.*

Paved areas

In very small gardens, where too much valuable planting space would be used up by a lawn, or in larger ones, where you want to create a different mood by making a garden "room" enclosed by a yew or beech hedge, an area of paving can be remarkably labor-saving as well as providing homes for little carpeting flowering plants.

If you have a small town garden with a deciduous tree, one way of dealing with the shady area beneath it is to lay paving. When preparing the soil and laying the paving (as described below) do not damage the tree's roots and be extra careful not to change the existing soil level around the trunk of the tree. The tree's roots will be happy underneath the stone slabs, and you can leave occasional spaces in the paving for suitable plants. Once established, *Dryopteris filix-mas* (the male fern), is remarkably tolerant of dry positions, and would look most appropriate. Periwinkle (*Vinca minor*), *Viola labradorica*, *Hypericum androsaemum*, Solomon's seal (*Polygonatum*) and ivy (*Hedera*) are more suggestions of plants that would thrive. You could arrange a specially large space for autumn cyclamen (*Cyclamen hederifolium*). Utterly hardy, its little pink and white flowers in the autumn are followed by leaves, beautifully marbled in silver-gray, that remain fresh and decorative all winter. A plant you can never have too much of, it will seed itself happily each year.

Planting between paving stones

The soil below the paving should be well drained and of good quality. First, level it and top with a 2 in. layer of sand. Leave spaces between the paving slabs of about 1½ in. and fill them with a mixture of two parts good soil, two parts sharp grit or horticultural sand and two parts leaf mold. Choose plants for sun from the list on page 37. Water the plants before taking them out of their containers and tuck their rootballs well down between the slabs. Make sure the stems and leaves of the plant are arranged nicely on the surface of the stone, so the plants will be able to sun themselves on the stone as their roots search beneath for food and moisture. Water well to settle them in. You might want to leave out a whole slab here and there, making in effect a mini-flower bed for a few larger plants.

Gravel surfaces

One way to solve the problem of lack of time to mow the lawn is to use gravel instead of grass: you get a similar effect of a wide expanse of space. In small shady town gardens, under the drip of trees where grass would not thrive, by using lots of evergreen shrubs and shade-loving plants you can make a cool retreat centered on an area of gravel, a private place in which to sit and dream. The tiny, creeping Corsican mint (*Mentha requienii*) would make a delicious minty smell at your feet (you might have to replace it after a hard winter).

Sunshine and gravel gardens mix just as well, and there are endless possibilities as the little stones act as a mulch and plants love growing in it. If you have lots of space to fill, make rainbows of thyme in mauve, purple, pink and white; or if you have run out of room to try out yet another plant—you may well find a place for it on the edge of a gravel path or drive. A planting plan for gravel in a shady position is given on page 38.

Planting in gravel

Prepare the soil for any flower bed (see page 81), then level it with a rake. To firm the soil, walk backward and forward with little shuffling steps, keeping your feet close together, all over the area. Rake the soil again, and remove any large stones. Plant any large

Making tapestries on the ground

Once you have prepared the soil (see above), put in any large plants and spread the chosen gravel, you are ready to create the effect you want from your planting. Arrange the plants, still in their containers, where you think they would look best. Think about color, seasonal interest, shape and height and try to achieve a balanced effect, but without formality. Stand back and look at the plants critically and make any small adjustments. Once you have placed the plants to your satisfaction, you are ready to begin planting.

Once you have firmed a plant in with soil, replace the top layer of gravel, tucking it carefully under the plant's leaves.

SUN-LOVING PLANTS

Acaena 'Blue Haze'

Alyssum saxatile citrinum

Arabis ferdinandi-coburgii

Armeria maritima

Artemisia schmidtiana 'Nana'

Artemisia stelleriana

Aubrieta deltoidea

Campanula cochlearifolia

Campanula portenschlagiana

Campanula poscharskyana

Chamaemelum nobile

Dryas octopetala

Erigeron karvinskianus

Erysimum 'Moonlight'

Geranium cinereum 'Ballerina'

Geranium sanguineum cultivars

Helianthemum

Hypericum olympicum uniflorum 'Citrinum'

Iberis sempervirens 'Little Gem'

Lobelia pedunculata

Phlox douglasii cultivars

Potentilla alba

Saponaria ocymoides

Saxifraga cotyledon

Thymus serpyllum cultivars

Trifolium repens 'Purpurascens'

ABOVE LEFT *Rock pinks (Dianthus 'Joan's Blood') are suitable small subjects for planting in gravel. They insist on full sun and a well-drained, slightly alkaline soil.*

trees and shrubs (see page 82) before spreading about 4–6 in. of small gravel or washed pebbles, such as you would put on a gravel driveway, and raking it level. Small-stoned gravel is best: larger stones are noisy and uncomfortable when walked on.

Arrange the plants to your satisfaction, as shown in the illustration opposite. Make sure that their roots are moist by watering them an hour or so before removing them from their pots. When planting a medium-sized plant, such as a hosta, scrape away the gravel in the chosen position and remove the plant from its container. Using a trowel, make a generous hole in the soil, larger than the plant's container, and loosen the soil at the bottom a little. Work in half a bucket of garden compost and a good handful of bonemeal. Put in the plant and top off with soil, firming gently as you go. Tuck the gravel under the foliage of the plant. With a very small plant, make a hole in the gravel, and raise the level of the soil 2 in. or so with good soil and then plant, leaving room for 2 in. of gravel topping on the surface. Using a watering can with a rose, water the plants in and wet the gravel as well, to wash off any soil.

Pots and tubs

You can be as daring as you like in your choice of plants for containers, for this is the place to grow plants that would look out of place in a border: exotic-looking tender plants like *Brugmansia*, tender *Fuchsia* cultivars such as 'Thalia,' pots of sumptuous *Lilium auratum* and *L. speciosum* var. *album*, pots of basil for tomato soup and an indispensable pot of lemon verbena (*Aloysia triphylla*) for the scent of its crushed leaves. By planting in containers, you have scope to use special soil mixes to suit plants that will not grow in your garden soil: if your soil has lime, by filling your pots with acidic compost you can still have pots of camellias and rhododendrons or, for once, have beautiful blue hydrangeas.

Pots and tubs of tender perennials and shrubs outdoors for the summer are joined by the throng of half-hardy annuals visiting for the season. The ambience of the terrace or paved area should be a cornucopia of plenty, with a profusion of plants spilling out of the pots. If these are small pots, group them all together, to give an impression of a tumbling mass of color and scent. When assessing the number of plants for a container, always over-estimate what you think you need. For example, a 14 in. diameter container could have five petunias, five *Verbena* 'Silver Anne' and two *Helichrysum petiolare*, while a large wooden tub 2 ft. in diameter could hold one *Canna*, three *Fuchsia magellanica* 'Versicolor,' three *Argyranthemum*, three *Plecostachys serpyllifolia*, seven petunias and seven verbenas. To keep tightly packed plants in the pink of health, they need regular doses of liquid feed.

In small gardens, where dying bulb foliage can be obtrusive, mass them in pots on the terrace or patio. Seen here is a generous planting of annual tulips, predominantly Tulipa 'White Triumphator,' and small pots of herbs. For more information on planting containers for spring, see page 106.

A shady town garden with gravel

Make sure the soil beneath the gravel is clean and incorporate plenty of humus before inserting plants as described on page 36. Spread the gravel over the whole area—it will unite the scheme and act as a mulch for the plants. Add containers of lilies, *Impatiens* and *Nicotiana* for summer color and, for a touch of formality, balls of clipped box. Allow *Mentha requienii* and *Lobelia pedunculata* (a prostrate mat with tiny blue flowers) to spread around in the central area.

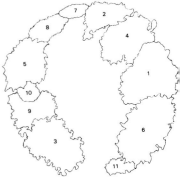

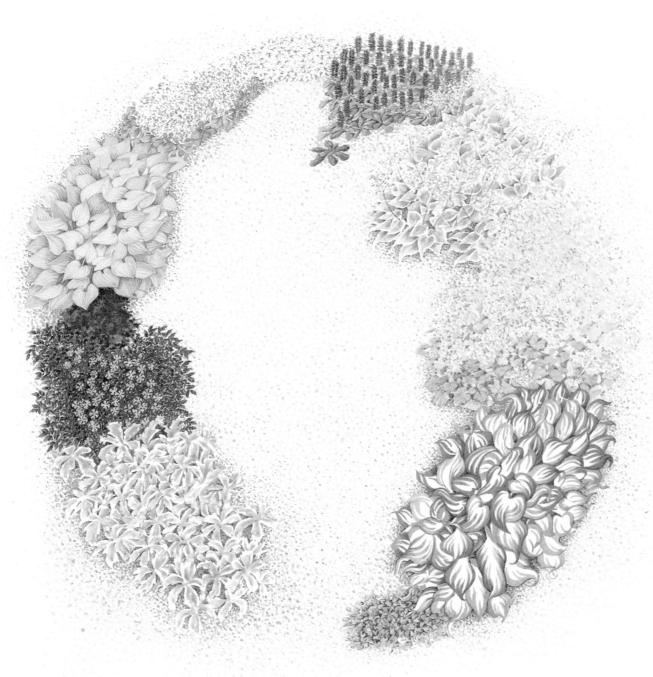

1 *Alchemilla mollis*
2 *Ajuga reptans* 'Atropurpurea'
3 *Astrantia major* 'Sunningdale Variegated'
4 *Brunnera macrophylla* 'Hadspen Cream'
5 *Hosta* 'Halcyon'
6 *Hosta undulata* var. *univittata*
7 *Lamium maculatum* 'Beacon Silver'
8 *Saxifraga × urbium*
9 *Vinca minor*
10 *Viola cornuta*
11 *Viola labradorica purpurea*

All the plants in this gravel garden, seen here in early summer, would enjoy their shady position and will spread happily around. Their quiet, cool shades are appropriate for a shady patch and form a good background for pots of summer color.

A *bed of exotic-looking plants*

It is easy to play safe and make lovely soft arrangements of plants using lots of gray foliage and pastel colors, but occasionally it is fun to be more adventurous and invent a dashing scheme of tender perennial and annual plants with a tropical look, making good use of striking foliage.

This exciting experiment with foliage contrasts and exotic-looking flowers would be decorative for three months, with a climax in late summer.

1 *Alonsoa warscewiczii*
2 *Amaranthus caudatus* 'Viridis'
3 *Arundo donax*
4 *Canna indica* 'Purpurea'
5 *Eucomis bicolor*
6 *Hibiscus trionum*
7 *Melianthus major*
8 *Nicotiana langsdorfii*
9 *Nicotiana* 'Lime Green'
10 *Ricinus communis* 'Impala' (N.B.: poisonous)
11 *Verbena × hybrida* 'Tropic'

Other plants you could use to extend the bed:
Bidens ferulifolia
Cordyline australis purpurea
Cosmos atrosanguineus
Dahlia 'Bishop of Llandaff
Euphorbia marginata
Mimulus aurantiacus
Molucella laevis
Rudbeckia hirta 'Marmalade'
Sanvitalia procumbens
Zinnia 'Envy'

Creating height

A new garden can sometimes look very flat, as nothing has had time to grow to a reasonable height. One of the ways around this is to put up an arch, or a series of arches forming a tunnel, some trellis-work in metal or wood, or to do things in the grand style and build a pergola. These partitions prevent you from seeing the whole garden in one glance. They can camouflage a utilitarian part of your plot and at the same time provide a home for all the lovely climbers you want to grow. If you are in a hurry for height at the beginning, rather than plant a quick-growing tree that could soon cause its own problems by starving the surrounding soil or casting too much shade, try training a large-leaved ivy up a pole for an immediate effect.

A note about trellis: the ready-made wooden trellis, that you can buy in sections, is often as flimsy as it is cheap, and is only strong enough for fixing onto a wall. Even then, a too-vigorous climber can cause the whole trellis to fall down in a gale. Clothed with foliage, trellis acts as a sail in the wind and needs to be supported at 6½ ft. intervals with strong supports, preferably bedded in cement.

A clematis trained up a pole is a marvelous way of introducing a contrast in height. By surrounding the pole with a sleeve of large-gauge wire netting you give the clematis something to cling to. Clematis 'Hagley Hybrid' is seen rising above foxgloves, roses and large patches of Astrantia major *and* Geranium endressii.

A quick-growing screen

A young garden has no little surprises or secrets around corners. Just a blank canvas of bare earth, it can seem remarkably empty before your long-term plantings, with all their different heights and shapes, give interest and depth to the picture. So, for the first summer, try using annuals planted on trellis, arches or poles. If you erect a simple, temporary screen (made of chicken wire or plastic-covered wire mesh supported by stout stakes) in different places in the garden, you will have a good opportunity to observe where some height would be appropriate in the long term.

For a sunny position, sweet peas (*Lathyrus odoratus*) might be your first choice as an annual screen, the epitome of summer with their gentle colors and nostalgic scent. They require what is known in horticultural terms as "a deep, rich root run." This means double-digging to two spades' depth, or 2 ft. deep, with generous helpings of rotted manure or compost worked into the lower portion of the hole and a general fertilizer mixed into the top layer, making a crumbly, loose mixture through which the roots can run freely. If you are prepared to forego the larger, frillier flowers of the modern sweet peas, try growing the smaller-flowered but richly fragrant 'Painted Lady,' a carmine and white bicolor that has been in our gardens for the last two centuries. Sweet peas make such a delightful flowery curtain that you can hardly bear to pick them, but if you do not they will soon set seed and give up flowering.

A wigwam of runner beans is easy to make out of tall bamboo canes wired firmly together at the top. It takes up surprisingly little room, adds useful instant height, does not look out of place in the flower border with its red or white flowers, and of course supplies a delicious vegetable for the kitchen. Beans like the same rich soil as sweet peas, and to keep them in full production they must be regularly picked while still young and tender.

Cobaea scandens is a splendid performer in the short space of a summer, with its large and bell-shaped flowers, shaded from palest green to wonderful sinister purple. It will wind its way up a fence or scramble up a wall in no time and will bloom till late autumn. It is simple to grow, provided you remember that it comes from subtropical America and likes both warmth and shelter. In the wild it is a perennial and in very mild climates will behave accordingly.

The twining golden hop (*Humulus lupulus* 'Aureus') will rapidly add a bright patch of yellow foliage to a young garden and is an ideal plant for clothing a new summer house or pergola. It is not an annual but a herbaceous perennial that comes up anew from the ground each year. All it requires is any garden soil.

Climbing nasturtiums (*Tropaeolum majus*), so common and so cheerful, are wonderful fillers for the first year, especially on poor soil; too rich a mixture will encourage them to lush growth and few flowers. The canary creeper (from Peru), *Tropaeolum peregrinum*, a more refined plant with lemon-yellow, slightly frilly flowers, can be planted near a shrub that has finished flowering. Once you have had it in the garden, odd seedlings will unexpectedly turn up here and there.

Purple bell vine (*Rhodochiton atrosanguineus*) has enchanting darkest purple little trumpet flowers, suspended from pale crimson calyces that continue to decorate the twining stems after the blooms are over. Although it looks far more difficult than it actually is, this tender plant does need starting off in warmth from seed and to be given a very sheltered place outside for the summer. It sets seed sparingly and you will have to hunt around in autumn to find the odd ripe seed capsule.

One of the first packets of seed to order will be one of Chilean glory vine (*Eccremocarpus scaber*). It has ferny leaves and tubular flowers in orange, cherry red, yellow—or sometimes pink. It takes up little room as the stems seem almost weightless and you could plant it to grow up through your most valuable shrub. Furthermore, it seems quite happy in starvation conditions at the foot of a sunny wall. In milder areas it is perennial but elsewhere you can start it again from seed (if it has not already seeded itself).

Morning glory (*Ipomoea* 'Heavenly Blue') has unbelievable dazzling blue funnel-shaped flowers. You will want to go out every morning to count them. If you buy plants, be careful not to plant them out too early in the summer, for a chill at this stage will make the foliage turn pale and sad, and the plants will take weeks to recover. And if you start them off yourself in warmth, make sure they are carefully hardened off. Sun, shelter from cold winds and regular watering are required.

If you are wondering whether or not to plant a hedge in a particular place in the garden, you can see what it would look like by planting a row of Jerusalem artichokes (*Helianthus tuberosa*). If you do not like the effect by autumn, you can dig up the tubers over the winter and make them into soup. Jerusalem artichokes are not too fussy about soil, will grow up to 10 ft. and will make a useful summer windbreak.

*Wisteria (*Wisteria floribunda *'Alba') is an excellent climber to train over a pergola. After flowering, the attractive ferny foilage will form a shady arbor. For pruning wisteria, see page 65.*

Focal points

BELOW LEFT *A clipped* Prunus lusitanica *forms a living focal point at the end of this path dividing flower borders in pastel colors (with* Onopordum acanthium *in front).*

BELOW RIGHT *An arch swathed in* Rosa *'Adélaïde d'Orléans' frames the view of a stone seat. Black-eyed* Geranium psilostemon *and pink* G. endressii *spill over the path.*

Every garden needs some focal points to lead the eye and these can be deliberately placed—like a seat or a statue—or natural, such as an inviting woodland path disappearing around a bend. On a small scale they can simply be a handsome pot. You can use a plant to act as a full-stop, for example, an upright juniper (*Juniperus communis* 'Hibernica') or a fastigiate golden yew (*Taxus baccata* 'Fastigiata Aurea'). An architectural plant with bold spiky leaves, like a variegated *Yucca*, silvery *Astelia* or one of the New Zealand phormiums will also draw the eye.

Sometimes you visit a garden and a very busy, agitated picture presents itself. The owner probably started off with a well-placed seat, the effect was delightful, and then he or she went on adding more

focal points and plants with bright, eye-catching foliage. The result is a kaleidoscope of color with a squad of statues, a vast accumulation of plants and everywhere a pot, an urn or a seat. Each plant or artifact may be beautiful in itself but one is breathless trying to take it all in. So something else to remember when planning your garden is the fine line between too little visual stimulation and too much.

As white-painted garden furniture can dominate the view by looking too self-important, try toning it down with dark green paint mixed with liberal additions of black. Stark, new terra-cotta flower pots will quickly mellow and attract algae and moss if you paint them with a mixture of manure, water, milk and liquid general fertilizer.

Flowers for cutting

Cutting gardens, consisting of rows of flowers grown only for picking, originated in the walled gardens of grand country houses. They conjure up an image of the lady of the house making little excursions there in the cool of the early morning, wearing a straw hat and carrying a basket. There she could pick and pick, to her heart's delight, great armfuls of sweet peas, lilies, peonies and border carnations by the hundred.

But with a little imagination and a small bunch of flowers from the supermarket, you can invent something lovely—provided you have planted some suitable leaves in your garden. It is always easy to buy the larger flowers—chrysanthemums, tulips, gladioli, carnations and so on—but usually impossible to get the pretty fillers-in, such as *Alchemilla*, *Aquilegia*, *Heuchera*, fennel (*Foeniculum*), *Tellima*, *Astrantia*, Queen Anne's lace (*Anthriscus sylvestris*) and *Tanacetum* (formerly *Chrysanthemum*) 'White Bonnet'—which are essential for a softening effect. They will hardly notice a snip here and there (unlike some flowers that I would not pick—tree peonies, for example). Here is an *aide-mémoire* of suitable flowers for cutting each season. A list of flowers grown for their seed heads may be found on page 87.

Among the most useful plants to grow for their decorative foliage are: *Arum italicum italicum*, *Bergenia*, *Elaeagnus*, *Eucalyptus*, *Euphorbia robbiae*, *Euonymus fortunei* 'Silver Queen' and others, *Heuchera micrantha* 'Palace Purple,' *Hosta*, *Pittosporum*, *Ruta graveolens* 'Jackman's Blue,' *Skimmia* and *Sarcococca*.

Spring

Convallaria

Doronicum

Helleborus

Jasminum

Narcissus

Tulipa

Early summer

Astrantia

Aquilegia

Hesperis

× *Heucherella*

Polygonatum

Summer

Agapanthus

Antirrhinum

Alchemilla

Allium

Alstroemeria

Anthemis

Argyranthemum

Aster

Astrantia

Campanula

Cosmos

Delphinium

Dianthus

Digitalis

Foeniculum

Gypsophila

Hydrangea

Lathyrus

Lilium

Malva

Molucella

Paeonia

Papaver

Phlox

Romneya

Rosa

Selinum

Thalictrum

Tanacetum

Verbena

Late summer and autumn

Anaphalis

Aster

Dahlia

Dendranthema

Gladiolus

Nerine

Rudbeckia

Schizostylis

Sedum

Solidaster

Allium aflatunense will seed itself provided you do not pick off all the flowers to use in the house.

PLANTING FOR EFFECT

Gardening with flowers is like trying to control a picture in which most of the components change their appearance daily. Making a flower garden is not just a question of accumulating a quantity of flowering plants; however lovely each is individually, you are merely assembling a collection. With the multiplicity of wonderful plant material at our disposal, good planting is the juxtaposition of your own selection into a satisfying whole. As you experiment with plants, with a resulting mixture of glaring mistakes and heady surprises, you will find that there is no limit to their unpredictability.

The massed planting of Anemona blanda, *seen here beneath* Rosa glauca *(not yet in leaf), creates a dramatic effect in spring.*

The principles of good planting

Deciding where to plant something involves thinking of shape, size, habit, color and texture all at once. Every new plant you add to an existing flower bed changes how everything else looks. For example, a tall plant will seem taller if surrounded by a low carpeting plant. One with sword-like leaves will look spikier if grown next to a fluffy, mounded plant and a plant with blue flowers will seem a more intense blue if planted next to one that is silver-gray.

Add to this all the plant's likes and dislikes. Does it like sun, or shade, dry or moist conditions? When does it bloom, and for how long? Has it got an off-season, like *Colchicum*, which die an untidy death in midsummer? This flood of necessary information about a plant may seem too much at the beginning. But the more you understand about a plant, the better you are able to place it to good effect.

It is important to find out all you can about any plant at the outset. (Latin names are the same worldwide, so once you know a plant's correct Latin name it is easy to look it up.) If you know where a plant comes from in the wild, you will get some clues as to how to grow it properly. However perfectly something is placed with regard to color or form, if it will not thrive where you plant it, you defeat the object. If it comes from a Himalayan glade with high rainfall it will not like the hot, sunny position chosen for your Mediterranean plants.

Furthermore, plants from widely differing native habitats make uncomfortable bedfellows: dahlias interplanted with rhododendrons would strike a discordant note. How much more harmonious the rhododendron bed would seem if late-flowering lilies, gentians, *Kirengeshoma*, toad lilies (*Tricyrtis*) or some lacecap hydrangeas had been used instead. Reveling in the same coolness at the root and moist, acid conditions as do the rhododendrons, they would seem entirely appropriate. And dahlias, gorgeous pouting beauties as they are, also have their proper place in the garden—with lavish helpings of manure to nourish their splendid blooms and bright sunshine to remind them of their native Mexico.

Ease of transplanting

Find out if a plant you are considering is the sort of plant that has to be put in the right place first time, as it will not tolerate being dug up and moved, such as *Baptisia* or burning bush (*Dictamnus albus*). Or perhaps it is a gypsy plant that does not mind, indeed enjoys, being constantly on the move? As you shuffle the components of your flower beds around, adjusting the colors, reorganizing the heights and filling the empty spaces, it is good to get to know all the tinker fraternity—*Geranium*, *Campanula*, *Phlox*, and countless different members of the daisy family —that are the backbone of the herbaceous border.

The striking purple leaves of Ricinus *and* Canna, *backed by the airy foliage of* Rosa moyesii, *accentuate the pompon shape of the dahlias and the flower spikes of* Kniphofia.

LEFT *Juxtaposition of shape and habit is easy to understand in this restricted color scheme: tall spires of* Asphodeline lutea *and trumpet flowers of* Hemerocallis *'Golden Chimes' throw into relief the large, corrugated leaves of hostas and the scalloped foliage of* Alchemilla mollis.

Shape and texture

**Paeonia obovata
var. *alba***

*This herbaceous perennial
peony, with its fleeting
single flowers lasting but
a few days in early
summer, is native to
China and Siberia. In
early autumn there is a
second season of beauty as
the seed heads split open to
reveal a striking pattern
of seeds, some navy blue,
some scarlet. The former
are the fertile ones, which
should be sown as soon as
they are ripe and firm.*

It is easy to be blind to the shape and texture of a plant by being totally preoccupied with the beauty of its individual flowers—just like being so dazzled by a person's face that you do not notice his or her figure. The shape of a plant, or even the lack of it, is of primary importance and its texture is a determining factor in where it is placed. So before thinking about flower color, always consider foliage and form.

Plant shape

"Habit" is a word used in gardening books to explain to the reader roughly how a plant behaves, and a plant's habit largely determines its shape. What does it do, and how, when and how fast does it do it? If a plant grows straight up in the air, like an Italian cypress, it is what is known as "fastigiate" in habit. It may be pendulous in habit, like a weeping willow, or may creep along the ground, as does *Hyperium olympicum minus*, closely draping itself over stones.

Good gardeners, like good cooks, seem to know instinctively how, and in what proportion, to mix the ingredients. If you have an existing flower bed that you are not happy with, consider whether it needs the addition of a spiky-leaved plant, or more plants of rounded shape, or a strong, upright feature to improve matters. Or perhaps the planting seems too solid, and needs to be lightened by the addition of plants with delicate, lacy foliage. Often a simple planting of a decent patch of *Bergenia*, or plain-leaved *Hosta*, will soothe the eye. If on the other hand you have a new garden with an empty flower bed, buy several plants together and try them out in different places, still in their containers, and juggle them to see how they look next to each other.

The most distinctive plant shapes (below) all have a role to play in the total picture:

Spiky plants, with sword-like leaves like *Yucca*, *Phormium*, *Astelia* and *Kniphofia caulescens*, arrest the eye and form a definite full-stop in a flower border. They form an essential contrast to the softer mounds and hummocks of other plants.

Large plain-leaved plants, such as *Bergenia* and *Hosta*, greatly simplify the effect of massed herbaceous flowers when planted in groups. Most herbaceous subjects are meadow plants in the wild where, in order to survive crowded competition, their flowering stems reach up toward the light. Their scruffy shape and form is much improved when they are associated with positive, bold leaves.

Ferny, lacy leaves are another element in the foliage orchestra. They characterize plants such as

Five distinctive plant shapes

The majority of plants for the flower garden can be broadly grouped according to these five categories. It will help you to plan your planting if you see your chosen plants fitting within these groups. You can alter or improve the effect of an existing bed, too, when you review it in terms of plant shapes. The addition of one plant or a group of plants can lighten, dramatize or just pull together the plantings you already have.

*Spiky plants form an
essential contrast.*

*Large, plain-leaved
plants can provide relief.*

fennel (*Foeniculum*), *Astilbe*, *Thalictrum*, *Selinum tenuifolium* and, of course, ferns themselves.

Rounded hummocks, of plants like *Santolina*, *Artemisia*, small *Hebe*, lavender (*Lavandula*), sage (*Salvia*) and rue (*Ruta*), make gentle mounds without which a composition could look too busy.

Vertical accents are the final component, without which the picture will always seem incomplete. Plants such as the Irish juniper (*Juniperus communis* 'Hibernica') or Irish yew (*Taxus baccata* 'Fastigiata') make an important statement. In a small flower bed a conical, clipped box (*Buxus*) serves the purpose.

Plant texture

The different textures of foliage to weave into your picture are limitless, and besides the shape of each plant, try to keep in mind how to contrast their textures to best effect. Some leaves have such tactile quality that you cannot wait to handle them—the great white woolly leaves of *Salvia argentea*, the silver velvet of *Stachys byzantina* (lamb's ears) or the smooth gray plush of *Origanum dictamnus*, a delightful, somewhat tender origanum from Crete. There are shining leaves of plants such as *Bergenia* and *Camellia* that catch the light and throw it back to you, bristly

leaves (as if they have forgotten to shave) of *Symphytum*, borage (*Borago*) and *Anchusa* and the handsome, rough wrinkled foliage of *Rodgersia*. To complete the picture, there are fleshy, succulent leaves, those with thorns and prickles, and young, tender leaves that it would be a sin to squeeze.

Without the spiky foliage of the Phormium *(right foreground) and the tall* Persicaria *and variegated grass (left), this bed would be much blander.*

Ferny, lacy leaves will lighten a bed.

Hummocky plants provide a gentle note.

Vertical plants make an emphatic statement.

Size, balance and repetition

This lesson in good, balanced planting comprises dark green clipped yews for structure, large groups of plants (rather than small ones spotted around), repeating wide mats of Stachys byzantina, catmint (Nepeta) and pink Geranium endressii with contrasting spikes of Phaiophleps nigricans (formerly Sisyrinchium).

"Smallest in the front, tallest in the rear" is a rule that does not necessarily apply when planting a flower bed. An evenly graded bank of color can be viewed with one glance as the eye, easily bored, searches for something more. The occasional tall plant placed right in the front of a border can intrigue, particularly if it is the sort of plant you can see through, like *Verbena bonariensis*, growing to a height of 5 ft., or fennel (*Foeniculum vulgare*).

A gardening friend of mine says that people are often frightened of plants bigger than themselves, and this is understandable, but large perennials should not be avoided, even in the smallest garden. The new dimension of their extra height and the striking contrast they make with surrounding plants lifts the garden out of the mundane. And some plants simply demand a solitary position in the front of a bed, such as *Stipa gigantea* or angel's fishing rod (*Dierama pulcherrimum*), so as properly to display their graceful, arching wands.

Balance

Imagine a satisfying garden picture made up as follows: the highlights of each season take up the center stage, with a supporting cast of easy plants that can be tucked in around them, and all these plants are chosen because they are happy in your soil and conditions. Then, for the icing on the cake, there is an occasional rare or special plant that needs a little fussing over to thrive.

In the garden, just like anywhere else, the class system reigns. Some plants will only do well in first-class positions—the best soil going, the sunniest, or shadiest, spot, and so on. Every little whim must be attended to, whether it be dressings of fertilizer or manure, or regular spraying against any insect that would presume to attack. (And furthermore you may have to be ever ready with stakes, string and pruning shears.) Other plants, by no means less beautiful but nothing like so particular, will put up with the indignity of being put in any old corner, such as *Viola labradorica purpurea*, *Euphorbia robbiae*, *Erigeron karvinskianus*, *Geranium endressii*, moved when they are just about to flower and occasionally trodden on to boot, such as chamomile (*Chamaemelum nobile*) or thyme. So when you see some tempting new plant, make sure you can offer it the position it deserves.

Balance is the essence of planning your flower beds: however vibrant with color they are, if they only consist of a mass of bloom, with no background planting and foliage, no soothing patches of plain green leaves, the effect will be rather hectic. A good mixed border consists of one or two trees of character, a background of evergreen shrubs for structure, some flowering shrubs, herbaceous perennials, bulbs and ground-covering plants. Annuals and tender plants grown from cuttings each year complete the scene. While there is nothing to compare with traditional herbaceous borders on the grand scale, they do need a proper setting—walls of mellow brick, hedges of ancient yew or immaculate beech; also, to give of their best, they need to be of a decent width in the first place, ideally 10 ft. or more.

The low mounds of white Anaphalis triplinervis, repeated at the edge of both borders, unifies the planting and brings this whole scheme together. Yellow × Solidaster luteus and purple Phlox paniculata 'Harlequin' further coordinate the color theme used here.

In a small garden, often seen from the house, they can look like a large expanse of bare soil for months.

One of the enjoyable headaches of gardening is that however perfect a balance you achieve one year, you may be sure that by the next all will have changed: it is not like furnishing a room, when you can be quite confident that it will remain the same. In the garden the best-laid plans go awry: to redress the ever-changing shift in balance of color and size, and to prevent the overbearing behavior of one plant at the expense of another, vigilance is required.

Repetition

Most of us yearn to grow a little bit of this and that and quite a lot of the other, and irresistible new plants present themselves all the time. To begin with you will probably only have plants in ones and twos and dot them around an empty bed, giving it a busy, uncoordinated look. The simple trick of repeating the same plant several times down the length of the bed should simplify and soothe the overall effect. Purple sage (*Salvia officinalis* 'Purpurascens'), blue rue (*Ruta graveolens* 'Jackman's Blue'), *Artemisia* and dwarf red berberis (*Berberis thunbergii* 'Atropurpurea Nana') are suggestions for the front of a sunny bed. To add continuity to a shady bed, try *Hosta* (provided you use the same cultivar throughout) or, for a more formal bed, clipped box balls. As soon as your new herbaceous plants start to fatten up, divide everything that it is possible to divide, spreading out the pieces into drifts and groups, and the border will soon start to look more established.

When you are planning double borders, and want to form a repetitive pattern, stagger the plants down the length of each bed, rather than placing them exactly opposite one another. And, unless you are planning a very formal design (using something like box balls (*Buxus sempervirens*), do not place the plants exactly equidistant from one another.

Planting for year-round interest

Columbines (Aquilegia) are lovely plants for filling the gap between spring and summer, and can be persuaded to flower for longer if you dead-head them. Leave on one or two to seed themselves. The green flower-heads in the center are of Euphorbia robbiae, which will grow just about anywhere and is decorative for many weeks in spring.

In an ideal world, without limits of space, time, or money, one could have special gardens reserved only for bearded irises, for peonies, for Michaelmas daisies or any flowers, for that matter, that for a few radiant weeks would be looking their most glorious, and for the remainder of the year would be best forgotten. Hidden behind high walls, these gardens would be only visited in their prime. Imagine, for example, a winter garden, enclosed by cloisters, sheltered from the outside world, flagged in mellow sandstone in which one would only grow mimosa, the earliest camellias, scented tender jasmine (*Jasminum polyanthum*) and the lovely pale yellow *Coronilla glauca* 'Citrina.' There would be an ancient specimen of wintersweet (*Chimonanthus praecox* 'Luteus') in the center of the quadrangle, and from each corner the heady perfume of *Daphne bholua* would be carried on the air. A great quantity of the rare *Narcissus minor* 'Cedric Morris,' its little lemon-yellow daffodils

blooming on the shortest day of the year, would shine from the feet of the wintersweet. And in all the shady spots would be carpets of *Cyclamen coum*, whose flowers in white, pink and vivid magenta seem much too delicate to survive mid-winter.

Enough of this. Most of us have gardens far too small to indulge such fancies. A single border may have to contain all the different elements at once: something of interest in bloom most days of the year, something delicious to sniff, some scented leaves to crush and hold to one's nose, some patterned foliage, and an occasional rare and delectable plant in flower, to come upon by chance. The seductive curve of a petal, the sinister hood of an aroid or a billowing bank of shimmering color may enchant equally—but we would ideally like all these sensations at once, and in a very small space. There are several ways in which to assess the plants you choose to ensure that there is always something to look at in the borders.

Length of flowering

Always consider for how long a particular plant is going to contribute to your garden picture: does it have one brief moment of glory like an Oriental poppy (*Papaver orientale* cultivar) or bearded iris, or is it going to decorate the garden throughout the year with its eye-catching shape, like a yucca, that is highlighted in summer with spires of creamy bells? Some plants have flowers that are remarkably fleeting but they would still deserve a place, such as the exquisite single peony, *Paeonia obovata alba*, or the giant lily, *Cardiocrinum giganteum*. To help extend the season of interest in your flower beds, look at the list of plants that go on flowering (see page 55).

Self-seeders

Plants that seed themselves are a special bonus. Positioning themselves at random, in a spot you would never have thought of, they quickly soften the raw look of a new border. One can never have enough of the endearing little heartsease or wild pansy (*Viola tricolor*) or Venus' navel wort (*Omphalodes linifolia*), a confection of white and ice-blue. If you have a bed that has a muddled, disunited look, let *Campanula persicifolia*, the white musk mallow (*Malva moschata alba*) and *Tanacetum parthenium* scatter themselves here and there—they will often bring the whole thing together. Round up some of your foxgloves in early autumn and plant them together in groups to fill gaps. (You can tell whether foxglove seedlings are going to be pink or white by looking carefully at the base of the leaf stalks. If you just want white foxgloves, choose only those that are totally without a pink flush.) And do not forget columbines (*Aquilegia vulgaris*), equally happy in sun or shade, and one of the mainstays of the garden in early summer. As the columbines fade, toadflax (*Linaria purpurea*) will take over for the rest of the season. An immigrant from Europe that has come to stay for good, it will add a useful note of height with 3 ft. spires of tiny purple flowers.

Planting in layers

To make the best possible use of every bit of ground, always think of planting in layers: bulbs, their fading leaves masked by small, ground-covering plants and perennials, are complemented in turn by nearby shrubs, while an occasional small tree adds height. Climbing plants ramble on and up through each layer and, like painting a picture, you can add patches of color with annuals and biennials.

As you walk around the garden, instead of letting your eye glide from flower to flower in a haze of self-congratulation, search out critically any areas of bare soil, empty of color and interest. Perhaps the resident plants are late arrivals on the scene (in which case why have you not interplanted them with bulbs?) or they may, like Oriental poppies, have finished the summer season and are now having a rest. You can pull away their tired foliage (as you can with alstroemerias in later summer) and plant some late-sown annuals on top.

It is a race between you and nature as to who colonizes any empty soil first. There are a great many small plants—periwinkles (*Vinca*), *Alchemilla*, London pride (*Saxifraga × urbium*), *Viola labradorica* and *Cyclamen hederifolium* to name but a few—that are only too happy to be given a place under deciduous trees and shrubs, so plant some of these rather than let the weeds take over. And have a look at your trees and shrubs with a very circumspect eye—might they be suitable hosts for climbers?

Gardening is a much more cerebral occupation than you might think and you should always keep a notebook and pencil at hand (if it is raining a pencil will still work, a pen will not). Make notes about gaps in your borders and try to find out which plants of the season have been forgotten; consult books, visit other gardens and pester fellow gardeners with questions. Even make a surreptitious visit to the nearest nursery and buy plants in full flower if need be: though the plants might not give of their best to start with, at least this way you have a fine chance of getting the right plant in the right place first time.

SELF-SEEDING PLANTS
Anomatheca laxa
Aquilegia vulgaris
Campanula persicifolia
Hieracium maculatum
Hieracium villosum
Linaria purpurea
Malva moschata alba
Omphalodes linifolia
Onopordum acanthium
Papaver somniferum
Pseudofumaria lutea
Tanacetum parthenium
Verbena bonariensis
Viola tricolor

Flowers for every season

FLOWERS FOR LATE SPRING/EARLY SUMMER

Aconitum 'Ivorine'
Aquilegia
Asphodelus albus
Brunnera
Camassia
Convallaria
Dicentra many species
Dodecatheon
Euphorbia griffithii 'Dixter'
Glaucidium palmatum
Hemerocallis
   lilioasphodelus
Hesperis matronalis
Iris (dwarf bearded)
Lunaria rediviva
Mertensia pulmonarioides
Paeonia, many species
Podophyllum
Polygonatum
Ranunculus aconitifolius
   'Flore Pleno'
Ranunculus bulbosus
   'F.M. Burton'
Smilacina racemosa
Trollius in variety
Tulipa sprengeri
Uvularia
Veronica gentianoides

FLOWERS FOR AUTUMN

Aconitum carmichaelii
   'Arendsii'
Amaryllis belladonna
Anemone hupehensis
Anemone × hybrida
Aster
Boltonia
Cimicifuga simplex
Clematis heracleifolia
Colchicum
Cyclamen hederifolium

LEFT *For a successful border in autumn it is important to include late-flowering plants such as Sedum 'Herbstfreude' (with large pink flowerheads) as well as plants that are still looking good from earlier in the summer, as is lime-green Nicotiana and fennel (now going to seed but still decorative). The mauve-blue spikes (in the foreground) are the second flush of catmint (Nepeta) flowers, cut hard back after the first flush in mid-summer.*

RIGHT *Permanent planting for spring interest includes acid-green Euphorbia characias wulfenii and chartreuse E. polychroma (top left) with shiny-leaved Bergenia in the foreground.*

To be able to think sideways and around corners, in a lateral fashion, is a great help in gardening: optimists to the last, gardeners must always be thinking of next week, next year and ten years hence. And they need to be able to hold a picture in their mind's eye of what a plant is going to do, and at what time it will do it, and also take into account how its neighbors are going to behave. If you could only make a film of a flower bed, which ran constantly throughout the year, store it away in your head and play it back on demand, you would then see all the tricks that memory can play on exact recall of color, height and spread, let alone precise time of flowering of each individual flowering plant.

The seasons

Some seasons of the year will look after themselves: as the earth warms in the spring sunshine you can almost see things growing. Primroses in carpets and daffodils in drifts, streams of blue *Scilla, Chionodoxa* and *Muscari*, checkered fritillaries and erythroniums in little Turk's caps, tulips in flamboyant scarlet or elegant white—the soil seems to almost quiver with life and color. Early-flowering herbaceous plants appear in a surge of growth—bright yellow *Doronicum, Alyssum* and *Euphorbia polychroma, Pulmonaria, Lathyrus vernus* and many more—as winter pansies have their final fling and forget-me-nots make pools

of blue. Patches of *Anemone nemorosa* and celandines (*Ranunculus ficaria*) dot the ground under canopies of flowering cherries wreathed in blossom, while in spots reserved for the most exclusive plants, *Trillium* and bloodroots (*Sanguinaria canadensis*) hold court.

Then, as spring gradually fades into early summer there is a short interval, graced with every shade of fresh green you can think of, as summer's participants gather their strength and fatten their buds. Unless you are blessed with a lime-free soil for *Rhododendron*, *Menziesia*, *Phyllodoce* and other choice members of the Ericaceae, or a climate sufficiently mild to accommodate such Chilean beauties as *Embothrium coccineum*, you will have to be extra busy

with the notebook at this time. Three plants from the spring list on the opposite page deserve special mention for young gardens: *Aquilegia*, perennial honesty (*Lunaria rediviva*) and the double white sweet rocket (*Hesperis matronalis*). The first two are very easy from seed (and will seed themselves with alacrity in later years). Happily, the double sweet rocket, though rather hard to come by, is now available virus-free; its double flowers, scented toward evening, appear for months on end.

There is a moment when it seems time stands still, as the garden awaits the arrival of the sumptuous flowers of mid-summer—roses, bearded irises, delphiniums, peonies and Oriental poppies. Admittedly these plants need a little care to grow well, but who would be without them? The poppies do not need much attention, and the bit of ingenuity required to disguise the gap they leave after flowering is worth it for their silken, crinkled petals. Summer annuals will be starting their non-stop performance, continuing till autumn frosts, the high season for herbaceous perennials is just opening, and for a few short weeks the gardener is permitted to do a little sitting in the shade.

Late summer brings a tired and dusty feeling to the garden—hot winds and sun will have taken their toll on the freshness of spring; you must arise from your chair and sharpen both your wits and your pencil. The approach here is two-fold: the aim should be first to keep the plants that are flowering in pristine condition by dead-heading (see page 86), tidying and watering (see page 83), thus giving them every little encouragement to continue; and second, to incorporate a selection of plants that go on and on flowering.

Among the most cherished plants of the year are those that wait all summer and then put on a late display of bloom, when most other plants are getting ready for winter. Silver-leaved plants are at their gleaming best in the gentler light and many flowering grasses are at their peak in autumn. It is refreshing to discover something new in flower while rushing around tidying and reorganizing the plants.

FLOWERS FOR AUTUMN (continued)

Dahlia
Dendranthema
Eupatorium maculatum atropurpureum
Galanthus reginae-olgae
Lespedeza thunbergii
Leucojum autumnale
Liriope muscari
Nerine
Schizostylis
Sedum
Tricyrtis

PLANTS THAT FLOWER FOR A LONG TIME

Allium tuberosum
Aster × frikartii 'Mönch'
Aster × thomsonii 'Nanus'
Calamintha nepeta
Erigeron karvinskianus
Erysimum 'Bowles' Mauve'
Gaura lindheimeri
Geranium 'Ann Folkard'
Geranium × riversleaianum 'Mavis Simpson' and 'Russell Prichard'
Geranium wallichianum 'Buxton's Variety'
Knautia macedonica
Lavandula × intermedia 'Hidcote Giant'
Lavatera 'Barnsley'
Ononis rotundifolia
Osteospermum
Potentilla alba
Salvia 'Indigo Spires'
Viola (provided you deadhead them)

Plants to make a feature

Even the smallest garden needs the occasional theatrical plant with bold structure, if only to accentuate the difference between it and all the supporting cast that surrounds it. The stars of your garden picture will have all the more impact if they are not crowded out with other plants that have notions of stealing the scene. To form a backdrop, there is a vast range of humble plants that will melt into the background, quietly going about their business of growing, flowering and setting seed. Some of the most striking architectural, or feature, plants to make a dramatic impact are described below.

Onopordum acanthium (Scotch thistle, cotton thistle) is a giant silvery thistle, highly decorative and extremely prickly. Gloves are needed for weeding anywhere near it. It makes a spectacular silhouette of silver in a border in full sun. A biennial, in the first year it makes a spiny platinum rosette of leaves, and the following year a giant branching silver flower spike 8 ft. tall appears with pallid purple thistles on top: these duly scatter their seed, and the biennial cycle continues.

Symphytum × uplandicum 'Variegatum' (Russian comfrey) is a real show-off of a plant with handsome leaves brilliantly splashed in cream and soft green. Mauve-blue and cream flowers appear in summer on 3 ft. stems that are very pretty for a while, and when they start to look tired you should simply cut them down, along with any messy-looking leaves. In a few weeks the plant will be looking smart again. It is advisable to plant it in the right place the first time, because if it is moved, any portions of root that have been left behind will start to grow again, this time without the lovely variegation. It likes a rich diet and not too dry a position.

Ferula communis (giant fennel), the noblest of umbellifers, is a stupendous sight once it has built up the strength to send up its flowering stems 10 ft. high and more from a mound of finely cut leaves. Umbels of yellowish green flowers, like giant Queen Anne's lace (*Anthriscus sylvestris*), tower above surrounding plants. Native to the Mediterranean region, it likes plenty of sunshine. More suitable for the smaller garden is another umbellifer, *Angelica archangelica*, a handsome biennial with similar cow parsley flowers on 6 ft. stems. An architectural plant that likes rich soil, the flowers, stems and leaves are a symphony of green for a shady corner.

Gunnera manicata is a feature plant *par excellence*, but you do rather need a lake to go with it. It has enormous umbrella leaves and stems covered with prickles and minute greenish flowers in dense panicles. It needs rich, damp soil. It is one of the few plants equipped with its own winter protection—in autumn you can use its old umbrellas to wrap up the heart of the plant against frost.

Rheum palmatum 'Atrosanguineum' has large, deeply cut leaves like all the giant rhubarbs, and these could present a dramatic effect in the smaller garden. As the rich crimson-purple crumpled new leaves unfurl in spring, it is a highly exciting plant, all the more so as the flower spike begins to emerge. Panicles of soft crimson flowers atop the 6 ft. stem

In a silver and white border the dramatic silhouette of Onopordum acanthium *is outlined against a yew hedge, with* Rosa *'Iceberg,' white* Campanula persicifolia *and silver* Elaeagnus angustifolia *to the left.*

appear in early summer. Even after the flowers have faded, the handsome seed heads remain attractive till autumn.

Cynara cardunculus (cardoon) must be the queen of the silver plants, with its large, much divided, shining leaves, like the plumage of a giant silver bird. Luminous gray stems 6 ft. tall bear large blue thistle flowers in summer. You can get a similar, but less silvery, effect from the globe artichoke (*Cynara scolymus*). To keep the latter looking smart, keep pulling off any tired leaves. Both these plants need sun and well-drained soil. On a small, but highly exclusive, scale there is a rare little artichoke from Morocco, *Cynara histrix*, only 2 ft. high with gray leaves and baby artichokes flushed with shocking pink. Its requirements are the hottest position you can find and a pane of glass to protect it from winter rain.

Beschorneria yuccoides creates an exotic effect in the mildest gardens. It has beautiful long blue-gray spiky leaves and an incredible salmon-pink arching flower stem 7 ft. long, from which are suspended tubular green bells in early summer. If you do not dead-head it after the flowers fade, the old stems will remain decorative by retaining their lovely pink coloring for the rest of the season.

Veratrum is utterly hardy, with great personality both of leaf and flower, despite being very poisonous. Veratrums are so slow to establish you will have got to know them well by the time they have built up into large clumps, but they are well worth the wait. Their beautifully pleated leaves are neatly folded up like a fan as they emerge, a fresh and immaculate green, in spring. From then on, for the rest of the season, it is a battle with the slugs to keep them that way. *Veratrum nigrum* has tiny, purple-black flowers densely clustered on the flower spike; *V. viride* has racemes of bright green flowers; and *V. album* is white, washed with pale green. Veratrums do not need dividing very often and, as they like a rich diet, you should work in generous handfuls of bonemeal and compost or well-rotted manure around the plants occasionally, rather than move them.

Plants for small beds

For a small flower border the very same rules apply: try adding a small, bright gold *Hosta* like 'Golden Tiara,' or a group of *Celmisia* with spiky platinum leaves. The handsome, rounded leaves of *Darmera peltata* would do in a damp place if you do not have room for a *Gunnera*. Even the ordinary culinary fennel (*Foeniculum vulgare*) will become a star of the small screen if given an isolated position, surrounded by prostrate carpeting plants. In the magical light as the sun shines after a shower, when raindrops are caught in the fine silky foliage of the fennel, you may see a star being born.

Two eye-catching smaller plants with spiky leaves are *Iris pallida* 'Argentea Variegata' (blue flowers in early summer) and *Phaiophleps nigricans* 'Aunt May' (formerly *Sisyrinchium*). This latter has pale cream-striped leaves and spires of creamy-yellow flowers, forming a nice upright feature even in seed (to keep it looking smart you need to regularly trim away the dying leaves).

Euphorbia characias wulfenii, *a magnificent easy plant of great substance (with lime-green flower-heads, like frogspawn, in the center of the picture), adds character to any flower bed. It seems to fit into any sort of planting, among shrubs or herbaceous plants or even in the wilder parts of the garden. The bright pink flowers on the left are those of valerian* (Centranthus ruber).

Planting for color

Color is perhaps the most potent and exhilarating factor to play with in the garden. It is a deliciously complicated subject, not least because we use different words for the same color—what one person means by "pink" is the pale pink of a sugared almond, while to another it is the uncompromising, shocking pink of lipstick. And color is never static, changing constantly with the light. Soft and muted in early morning, by midday the sun bleaches out all pastel shades, and even the brightest colors lose some vitality. But by evening all the pale colors, white, palest yellow, pink and blue come into their own, and appear luminous in the shadows. On cloudy days, with only a hazy light, our gardens seem to ask for color schemes of silver foliage, flowers in soft, opalescent hues and leaves variegated with white.

Shimmering in the sun of hotter climates, the bright scarlets, vermilions, oranges and vivid yellows—colors that would dazzle in a low light—are of just the right intensity. And to miss out on this color range is to deny oneself the chance to experiment with the most exciting shades. Like difficult guests at a dinner party, they simply need some thought as to their placement. Not to invite such plants as the Maltese cross (*Lychnis chalcedonica*) because it insists on wearing startling red and is more than likely to have a confrontation with its neighbors is too fainthearted an approach. You could put it beside *Dahlia* 'Bishop of Llandaff,' with echoing scarlet flowers and rich bronze foliage, and *Heuchera micrantha* 'Palace Purple' and a carpet of *Verbena* 'Lawrence Johnston' in front; to further stimulate the company you could plant *Crocosmia* 'Lucifer' nearby.

When you first start to garden, it seems hard enough getting to know the plants, let alone thinking about color as well. But if you only start to consider arranging your colors after several years, umpteen plants will have to be transplanted. The simplest way to begin is to reserve one bed for soft colors, and another for all the strong, bright colors

The purple foliage of Heuchera micrantha *'Palace Purple' and* Berberis thunbergii *'Atropurpurea Nana' complements* Rosa *'Marlena' and* Verbena *'Lawrence Johnston.'*

often known as "hot" colors. When you get hold of a plant, put it into an imaginary file, labeled "soft" or "bright," and (taking careful notice of the plant's preferences regarding soil) place it accordingly. You may wish to define your ideas further by moving all the yellows and oranges to a bed of their own, and diluting them with blue flowers—*Aster × frikartii*, *Gentiana asclepiadea*, *Nepeta* and blue *Campanula*, *Aconitum* and *Viola*—and glaucous foliage—*Berberis temolaica*, *Ruta graveolens* 'Jackman's Blue,' sea kale (*Crambe maritima*), *Elymus magellanicus* and any *Hosta* with "blue" in its cultivar name, such as *Hosta* 'Buckshaw Blue' or 'Blue Moon.'

Making flower gardens based on one color—white, for example—is not simply a matter of looking up plant catalogs and ordering ten of every white flower you find on the list. The more restrained the range of flower color, the more important it is to interplant the flowers with complementary foliage plants, considering their shape and texture as well as

their color. Silver-gray *Stachys byzantina*, *Onopordum acanthium*, *Salvia argentea* and artemisias, together with glaucous foliage (see above) and cream-variegated leaves and, of course, many different shades of green itself, will create a white garden as opposed to a mere collection of white flowers.

These are not rules, only suggestions, and even these are there to be broken. Once you become aware of color, dashing and outrageous schemes will present themselves: try them out by picking a bunch of flowers in a certain color, sticking them in the ground where you are thinking of moving them to, and standing back to consider the effect. Just remember, as every flower arranger knows, that warm or hot colors (red, orange, bright yellow) advance and cool colors (blue, green) retreat; so, especially in a small garden, strong, bright colors are best placed near the house end, in order to increase the effect of distance, and cooler shades should be placed farther away.

A very limited color scheme can often prove the most successful. This border, in many different shades of cream through to yellow, includes the whorled flower-heads of Phlomis russeliana *(foreground), a cream-flowered* Anthemis tinctoria, Rosa *'Golden Wings,' white foxgloves and* Phaiophleps nigricans *(formerly* Sisyrinchium*).*

A border of hot colors

In this hot-color border, the cool tones of *Macleaya cordata* and *Alchemilla mollis* are included to further emphasize the rich bronze leaves of many of the plants—the chartreuse green of the alchemilla is particularly good with these dark tints.

The annual poppy, *Papaver somniferum*, with its pale sea-blue foliage and seedpods, should be allowed to seed itself here and there to prevent too studied an effect. Use plenty of crimson *Nicotiana* (you could use lime-green as well) to fill in while the other plants are small.

Other possibilities for compatible-colored plants include: *Euphorbia amygdaloides* 'Rubra,' *Cimicifuga ramosa* 'Atropurpurea,' *Canna indica* 'Purpurea,' *Lilium lancifolium* and *Lilium* 'Enchantment,' *Lychnis chalcedonica*, *Rodgersia pinnata* 'Superba,' *Rosa* 'Alexander,' 'Frensham,' or 'Marlena.'

This predominantly red border is seen in late summer, when all the different glowing reds (of Dahlia, Penstemon, Verbena, Nicotiana *and* Fuchsia) *enhance each other at their peak of flowering.*

1 *Alchemilla mollis*

2 *Ajuga reptans* 'Atropurpurea'

3 *Berberis thunbergii* 'Atropurpurea Nana'

4 *Beta vulgaris* (Ruby Chard)

5 *Cordyline australis purpurea* or dwarf bronze-leaved *Phormium*

6 *Cotinus coggygria* 'Royal Purple' (prune in spring if it gets too big)

7 *Crocosmia* 'Carmin Brilliant' or 'Lucifer'

8 *Dahlia* 'Bishop of Llandaff

9 *Euphorbia dulcis* 'Chameleon'

10 *Foeniculum vulgare purpureum*

11 *Fuchsia* 'Thalia'

12 *Heuchera micrantha* 'Palace Purple'

13 *Lobelia* 'Queen Victoria'

14 *Lobelia* 'Brightness'

15 *Lobelia* 'Dark Crusader'

16 *Macleaya cordata*

17 *Meconopsis cambrica flore-pleno*

18 *Nicotiana* (crimson)

19 *Penstemon* 'Chester Scarlet'

20 *Ricinus communis* 'Impala' (poisonous)

21 *Rosa glauca* (syn. *R. rubrifolia*)

22 *Verbena* 'Lawrence Johnston'

Flowering plants

Philadelphus *'Belle Etoile'* is one of the most appropriate shrubs for the flower border, blooming in early summer before the main display of herbaceous perennials. It is seen here with coral-pink Heuchera *and blue* Geranium.

The different sorts of plants at our disposal—flowering trees and shrubs, climbers, roses, hardy perennials, hardy annuals, tender perennials, biennials and bulbs—must each be considered according to their category. Flowering trees and shrubs could be divided into two files, one labeled "VIP, do not disturb" and the other "Disposable when it suits" (see this page). Climbers (see page 64) have special appeal to those with crowded gardens—there always seems to be room for another clematis. A rose (see page 72) can be chosen to suit almost any garden; their adaptability to different climates never ceases to amaze; *Rosa × odorata* 'Mutabilis,' for example, flourishes equally well in Dublin as in San Antonio, Texas, and Christchurch, New Zealand.

Hardy perennials have, as is their due, almost the whole of chapter 6, Key Plants, devoted to them (see page 108). By adding one or two structural evergreens one could make a brilliant flower garden of these alone. The frivolous element is provided by hardy annuals and tender perennials (see pages 73 and 74). These are the ephemera of summer, to play around with and to use in daring planting schemes

—even if they do not come off, you will have still had all the fun. Many biennials (see page 74), such as foxgloves, honesty or *Eryngium giganteum*, add joy by sowing themselves in the oddest places, while bulbs (see page 75) are essential to any flower garden as they beckon in spring and, in autumn, wave a final goodbye with *Colchicum*, *Nerine*, *Cyclamen* and autumn-flowering snowdrops.

Trees and shrubs

To form the background for your summer flowers, and to give shape and interest to the garden in winter, the first plants to decide upon are your structural evergreens. The plain, dark green of box (*Buxus sempervirens*) and yew (*Taxus baccata*), laurustinus (*Viburnum tinus*) and *Sarcococca*, *Viburnum davidii* and *Osmanthus delavayi* will never pall. The bright, spring green of some evergreens, *Griselinia littoralis*, for example, while quite acceptable in summer, is curiously disturbing in winter—perhaps subconsciously we only associate so fresh a green with spring.

Faced with an empty garden, the first instinct is to go out and buy a quantity of trees and shrubs. But as you patrol the lines of plants at the garden center, have a serious think before putting your hand in your purse: the agony of digging up something because it is squashing everything in sight or is not nearly as pretty as you thought is worth considerable trouble to avoid. As you have read in the chapter on planning the flower garden, a more useful approach is to decide at the outset which are going to be your important trees and shrubs, those that no other plant is going to interfere with in any way, and to plant beside them some easy, short-term fillers—short-lived shrubs (see page 32) and easily moved herbaceous plants and annuals—that you will not mind sacrificing after a few years.

Another consideration is to find out which plants respond well to pruning—it is not for nothing that yew, box and holly have been beloved by centuries of garden designers, as regular assaults on their twigs and foliage leave them quite unconcerned. *Choisya ternata*, growing 6–10 ft. high, can be kept to 5 ft. by pruning, a most enjoyable operation accompanied by the delicious spicy scent of the cut leaves and stems. *Fuchsia*, pruned by frost in cold gardens, can be treated as you like in mild areas—you have a choice of letting them assume tree-like proportions against a wall, or alternatively you can cut them to the ground in spring. *Pyracantha* can be allowed to grow into a large evergreen buttress, thus providing comfortable homes for nesting birds, or can be tightly clipped to a wall, better to display their sprays of creamy blossom and bright berries. *Buddleia davidii* positively *must* be pruned hard in spring, otherwise you get a lanky, jack-in-the-beanstalk effect, and you would not see the butterflies that so love its flowers—they would be hovering way above you.

One can never tire of the divinely pretty foliage of *Rosa glauca* (syn. *R. rubrifolia*), a sort of rosy-mauve with a bloom on it, on purplish stems. If you are prepared to sacrifice its single soft mauve-pink flowers with crimson hips to follow, and cut it nearly to the ground each spring (giving it a generous feed to make up), it can be treated just as a foliage plant—the leaves, even more richly tinted on 4–5 ft. stems, will make beautiful harmonies with any color scheme you have in mind.

But you do have to know which shrubs you can take liberties with—even to approach a *Magnolia*, *Daphne*, *Cornus* (except the sort grown for their colored winter stems) or witch hazel (*Hamamelis*) with shears would be a sort of horticultural sacrilege. (But one is permitted to give a very cautious trim to *Daphne cneorum* in order to keep it neat after flowering.)

From mid-summer on, the flower garden will be a banquet of scent and color, as perennials and annuals take the center stage. The flowering of *Carpenteria californica* and Californian tree poppy (*Romneya coulteri*) will be eagerly anticipated; both are aristocrats among flowering plants. These stand in their own right as stars of their season, but for your main

background planting you might consider using winter-flowering shrubs—the lovely pale yellow *Mahonia* × *media* 'Underway,' *Daphne bholua*, *Viburnum farreri* or *V.* × *bodnantense* 'Dawn,' *Jasminum nudiflorum*, and the compact *Viburnum tinus* 'Eve Price' with buds of bright pink. Particularly if you are the sort of gardener who shuts the garden door at the end of autumn and would not dream of going out again until the first signs of spring, these essential shrubs of winter will both furnish the garden and give the impression to anyone looking out of the window that you have made an effort.

The smaller the garden, the more thought you should give to leaf color when choosing shrubs. The right foliage color, aptly placed, can transform a quite ordinary flower bed into something special. Decide what sort of color scheme you would like, and pick something that will enhance your ideas. A bed of flowers in pale colors, soft pinks, mauves and primrose yellow would ask for silver foliage, while a range of scarlet, orange and strident yellow would positively gleam with vibrancy by the addition of shrubs in bronze and purple hues.

Carpenteria californica, which first flowered in the U.K. when planted by Miss Gertrude Jekyll at Godalming in 1885, could be one of your first choices of flowering shrub for a sunny wall. Well-drained soil and not too much rich feeding is required.

Climbers

If you think of your garden only in terms of how much ground it consists of, and how many plants you can possibly fit into the area available, you may be forgetting the wonderful amount of empty space that lies above the ground, that is yours to fill with beautiful flowering plants that climb. These plants may grace your walls, ramble through trees, entwine themselves through shrubs, tumble from banks and drape themselves in graceful swags from arch or trellis or pergola. They may even be planted on the flat in the flower border, where they will soon adapt to a new life at ground level. Little purple bells of *Clematis viticella*, planted to grow over a prostrate juniper or a patch of winter-flowering heather, can provide summer entertainment, or plant *Clematis* 'Perle d'Azur' to climb through *Cotoneaster horizontalis* 'Variegatus' for a pretty effect of cream and green leaves embroidered with blue flowers.

The first important thing to know about growing clematis is never, on any account, to lose the label. It is essential to remember the name of the particular species or cultivar so that you can check how it should be pruned (see page 89). Some of the large-flowered clematis require little pruning (just the odd tidying of dead or weak stems), while others that flower later in the season are cut down to about 3 ft. in late winter. *Clematis viticella* cultivars are also cut hard back at the same time. If you are planting a clematis to grow through a delicate shrub, remember that the host plant will need its annual release from the weight of clematis stems, so you should choose a clematis that needs hard pruning. And if you are growing clematis up walls, a useful way to support them is by fixing wire netting (chicken wire, quite large gauge) onto the wall—this weathers quickly and is not too intrusive.

Growing climbers up trees

The romantic idea of growing climbers such as roses and clematis up trees needs a little thought: if you dig a small hole near the trunk of a healthy, established tree, hastily shove in a young plant just out of its container, and forget to water it all summer, do not be surprised if it languishes and

LEFT *Honeysuckle (Lonicera periclymenum) is seen twining up a pergola. This is a useful fragrant climber for covering old tree stumps, training on walls or fences or disguising ugly buildings. Prune after flowering to keep within bounds and thin out any old wood.* BELOW LEFT Clematis *'Comtesse de Bouchaud' climbs up an apple tree. (This cultivar is a particularly good choice if your clematis are prone to clematis wilt.) Prune to 3 ft. in spring.*

finally dies. To give it a chance in life, dig a really decent-sized hole (3 ft. square and 2 ft. deep) several feet out from the base of the tree. Work in all the compost and manure you can spare and fill it up with good soil. Some support will be needed to guide the young plant into the tree. Copious watering during summer will help to redress the balance between the climber and its more forceful host. (See page 71 for advice on which climbing roses to grow up trees.)

Covering a large expanse of wall

One of the few flowering climbers that will do well on a north wall is the climbing hydrangea (*Hydrangea anomala petiolaris*). Although it is vigorous once established, it can be dispiritingly slow to get started, as it is easy to forget how dry the soil can be in such a place. So the better you look after it in the early stages, with generous watering (2 gallons twice a week) and feeding, the quicker you will be rewarded with its beautiful corymbs of sweetly scented, lacy flowers. The new leaves, unfolding into a fresh spring green early in the year, and the flaking warm brown bark of the mature stems in winter are little bonus points.

Clematis montana will festoon a large wall, pergola or old tree with its stems wreathed in late spring with white blossom. It must have plenty of room in the first place, because pruning it cuts off next year's flowers. (If you have inherited an old specimen that has turned into a tangle, you could give it a major cutback in early summer and let it start again.)

The true Virginia creeper, *Parthenocissus quinquefolia*, is a superb rampant climber that clings to walls with the tips of its sticky tendrils. As it has a cavalier attitude toward gutters and can easily bring them down with over-enthusiastic growth, try giving it its head by planting it against a tall tree. You will then be treated to the unforgettable sight of its leaves ablaze with crimson in autumn, backlit by the setting sun.

For a large sunny wall there is nothing more beautiful than a *Wisteria*, with long racemes of lilac blossom. Tempting as it is to let it cover the wall quickly, it must be properly pruned to encourage it to flower. In late summer cut all the young stems (except the one or two needed to build a framework) back to within 6 in. of the old wood, and do the same again in the winter to two or three buds.

Hydrangea anomala petiolaris *(feed and water well when young) is* draped with Tropaeolum speciosum. *This latter, often hard to establish, is ineradicable once it gets going.*

Some unusual climbers

Although you can never have enough clematis or, indeed, climbing roses, it is stimulating to give some of the more unusual climbing plants a chance. They might, of course, be more difficult to acquire, but you may well enjoy the challenge of tracking them down. All the following are easily grown, provided you choose them carefully to suit your soil and climate.

Calystegia hederacea 'Flore Pleno' is guaranteed to fool those who see it for the first time. The flowers look a little like pretty pale pink, slightly crumpled roses. But one glance at the leaves will remind you suspiciously of bindweed, and once you examine the plant a little closer and see its winding stems, the truth will dawn. For the double *Calystegia* is a close, albeit rather special, relative. But on account of its talent to amuse, you will probably forgive its wandering ways and uncontrollable behavior.

Dicentra scandens has flowers just like the bleeding heart (*D. spectabilis*). But instead of the rosy red or pure white of that much-loved spring flower, in this interesting climbing member of the fumitory family the late-summer flowers, massed together in little clusters among the ferny foliage, are a cool, lemon-green. It comes from the Himalayas and sets copious seed every year that seems hard to germinate (but although you would not expect that such delicate stems would root from cuttings, *D. scandens* is easy to propagate this way in early autumn). It seems equally happy on a sunny or shady wall, and as it dies to the ground each year you can dig it up and move it if necessary.

Aconitum hemsleyanum may not be the showiest of climbers, and it is only when you glimpse its brooding, helmeted, murky blue flowers suspended in the air above you that you can appreciate its quiet appeal. This climbing relative of the border monks-hoods is, like all its genus, very poisonous. But still it takes up little room, and can be left to entwine its way through a shrub or up bare stems of a lanky climbing rose.

A mild garden, a warm wall and a neutral or lime-free soil are required to grow *Billardiera longiflora*, a delightful twining plant from Tasmania. In summer

ABOVE *Several attempts may be needed to establish* Tropaeolum polyphyllum, *an interesting sprawling relation of the garden nasturtium. Full sun and good drainage are essential.*

LEFT Rhodochiton atrosanguineus *needs a protected site and would enjoy the shelter and reflected warmth of this old stone wall (see page 41).*

it has little greenish yellow bells that are followed in autumn by large, shining bright blue fruits. (You can also get forms with white or plum-red berries.) Its growth is delicate enough to allow it to ramble through choice small shrubs.

A gorgeous climber from Chile, *Berberidopsis corallina*, enjoys the same conditions but slightly alkaline soil can be adjusted to suit it by the liberal addition of organic matter. When it is happy, this climber can cover a large expanse of wall with evergreen foliage and racemes of beautiful pendent crimson blossoms in late summer.

If you have a very mild garden, one of the most exciting plants you can grow is *Bomarea caldasii*, in effect a climbing *Alstroemeria* (to which it is closely related). It spends the summer weaving its fleshy stems up its support on your hottest wall. In autumn, just when you think it is never going to bloom, umbels of brilliant orange flowers burst forth; the inside of some of the petals are spotted with crimson. You could also try the somewhat hardier *B. × cantabrigiensis*.

Codonopsis tangshen has flowers that are well camouflaged to the human eye, greenish bells fascinatingly veined with maroon and immensely attractive to wasps. If a buzzing noise reminds you to lift up a bell and look inside, you will be charmed with the intricate pattern therein, despite the foxy odor that is the signature of the genus. This is a long-lived, easy, herbaceous twining plant that does not need a place on a wall since it will insinuate itself happily up neighboring plants.

Codonopsis convolvulacea is an altogether different matter: a very beautiful plant, its fragile twining stems are so slender and so easily damaged that a choice spot, preferably in a shady raised bed should be chosen. As it disappears in winter, and does not turn up again until quite well on into the following summer, mark its position carefully and watch out for slugs. *Codonopsis convolvulacea* has large, open, bell-shaped flowers in mid-blue and there is also an exquisite white form.

There are some interesting perennial relations of the showy annual climber *Tropaeolum majus*, or nasturtium. There are *T. pentaphyllum*, with dainty little red and green flowers like elfin hats; blue-flowered *T. azureum*; and *T. tricolorum*, which is several colors all at once. These are all admittedly tender, but *T. tuberosum* 'Ken Aslet' is considerably hardier, especially when deeply planted under a sunny wall. It will rush up a wall and have a delightful summer affair with any nearby shrub, its bright orange-red flowers dancing about on their long stalks above the prettily lobed leaves. In colder areas the tubers (curiously marked with purple and reputed to be edible) may be lifted and stored.

Tropaeolum speciosum (flame nasturtium, Scottish flame flower) is a plant that is either the despair of those who wish to grow it, or else it grows with indecent abandon and swamps everything in sight —there seems to be no halfway measure. You may have to make several attempts to establish it, and although it is said to prefer acid soil, perhaps it is cool conditions and plenty of moisture that are the more essential. Although it can be a nuisance in a bed full of choice acid-loving plants, if you ever saw its dazzling little scarlet flowers trailing over a somber yew hedge, all would be forgiven.

Though still a comparatively scarce plant, Dicentra scandens *is a remarkably easy climber for sun or shade.*

A *flower border in soft colors*

In this sunny flower border of soft colors, nearly all the plants are easy to grow. To fill in gaps, when the plants are still young use *Campanula persicifolia*, *Tanacetum parthenium* 'White Bonnet,' *Eryngium giganteum* and white annual *Cosmos*. When the bed gets established and starts to become overcrowded, you can prune *Artemisia* 'Powis Castle' back hard in spring; if necessary you can give the *Brachyglottis* an

occasional major cutting back at the same time. Cut out the old flowering stems of the *Euphorbia* in late summer and prune the flowers off the *Brachyglottis* as soon as they fade. *Penstemon* are all the better for spring pruning, as is the *Perovskia*. If the bed is backed by a wall, *Cytisus battandieri* would be specially good with this color scheme.

1 *Achillea* 'Taygetea'
2 *Allium christophii*
3 *Anaphalis triplinervis*
4 *Artemisia canescens*
5 *Artemisia* 'Powis Castle'
6 *Aster × frikartii* 'Mönch'
7 *Aster thomsonii* 'Nanus'
8 *Brachyglottis* 'Sunshine'
9 *Calamintha nepeta*

10 *Dianthus* 'Doris,'
    'Constance Finnis,'
    'Gran's Favorite,'
    'Musgrave's Pink'
11 *Euphorbia characias
    wulfenii*
12 *Fuchsia* 'Tom Thumb'
13 *Galtonia candicans*
14 *Gladiolus* 'The Bride'

15 *Hosta* 'Halcyon'
16 *Iris pallida pallida*
17 *Iris pallida* 'Argentea
    Variegata'
18 *Kniphofia* 'Little Maid'
19 *Lilium regale*
20 *Limonium latifolium*
21 *Nerine bowdenii*
22 *Onopordum acanthium*

23 *Origanum laevigatum*
24 *Penstemon* 'Garnet'
    (this excellent old
    cultivar is now
    correctly called
    'Andenken an Friedrich
    Hahn')
25 *Penstemon* 'Evelyn'
26 *Perovskia* 'Blue Spire'

27 *Rosa* 'Margaret Merril'
28 *Rosa* 'Natalie Nypels'
29 *Sedum* 'Vera Jameson'
30 *Stachys byzantina*
31 *Thymus × citriodorus*
    'Silver Queen'
32 *Verbena rigida*
33 *Verbena* 'Silver Anne'
34 *Verbena bonariensis*

*In high summer the soft
pastel shades of this
flower bed are seen at
their best.*

69

ABOVE Rosa *'Felicia,'* one of the best of the hybrid musks, flowers for most of the summer. Regular dead-heading will keep the bush tidy and encourage further flowers.

RIGHT Rosa *'Graham Thomas'* looks wonderful in association with blue or purple flowers.

Roses

Who would be without roses? The quintessence of the summer flower garden, you may be equally as beguiled by the beauty of their appearance as by their heavenly scent. The names alone of the old roses are evocative, with their memories of nineteenth-century princesses, little-known French ducs and docteurs, généraux and maréchals, all the long-forgotten "blue blood" from the *Almanac de Gotha*. Gallica and Damask, Centifolia or Moss, Alba, China, Portland and Bourbon, climbing or rambling, shrubs—old-fashioned or otherwise—hybrid musks, hybrid perpetuals and what used to be hybrid teas (now large-flowered) and floribundas (now cluster-flowered) roses—and many more—how can one choose from such a sumptuous diversity?

Try to have a look at a rose in bloom, and see whether you like it or not. You may find, on looking it up by name, that it is "a weak grower," or "a martyr to blackspot," but you may well consider such a lovely thing worth slaving over with sprayer and liquid feed. The other criterion is, does it have a scent? It is so disappointing to sink one's nose into a bouquet of velvety petals and find nothing.

The modern large-flowered and cluster-flowered roses, often criticized for their gawky growth, are nonetheless good garden plants. With their cheerful willingness to flower over a long period, they deserve a place planted in small groups in the mixed border. Choose them in a color that complements their surroundings and plant some mounded, bushy plants nearby to help disguise their rigid habit.

But you may have lost your heart completely to the old-fashioned sorts (by this term I mean all but the modern large-flowered and cluster-flowered roses), in which case remember that many of them only flower for a few weeks. For the remainder of the summer they are rather uninspiring, dusty-green bushes. Invaluable for the small garden are those that are repeat-flowering or, like *Rosa × odorata* 'Mutabilis,' which is never out of flower from late spring to late autumn, or *R.* 'Graham Thomas,' a beautiful yellow modern rose but with all the attributes of an old-fashioned one, named in honor of the great plantsman and rosarian.

A word of warning: do make absolutely sure you have really fallen in love with a rose; it is no use taking it out and putting back one you think you like better in the same position. Specific replant disease is not just an old wives' tale: in some way the soil is poisoned by the roots of the discarded rose, and the new rose will remain sad and stunted (although other unrelated plants will not be affected). One solution is to change the soil to a depth of 2½ ft. or so.

Growing roses up trees

You will sometimes see *Rosa filipes* 'Kiftsgate' recommended for growing up a tree. It is indeed an incredible sight in full bloom, a tumbling waterfall of thousands upon thousands of creamy-white flowers in a great foaming mass. A Chinese species, described in the books as "vigorous," *Rosa filipes* is a monster rose of great beauty that grows with wild and rampant enjoyment, its new shoots reaching to 12 ft. in a summer. But what the books neglect to point out is that this rose has built-in special equipment for climbing through thick Chinese undergrowth—backward-pointing needle-thorns, barbed-like fishhooks that cling to anything nearby, from shrubs to large trees, with a special preference for passing human flesh. You might presume that you could control such a rampageous plant by pruning, but in order to do this you have to approach it, when one or more of its hooked talons will probably make a grab for your hair. Such an untameable rose should be given a large garden and masses of space to make a beautiful, but impenetrable, thicket.

Consider instead *Rosa* 'Albéric Barbier' (creamy yellow), 'Albertine' (pink), 'Rambling Rector' (white), 'Cécile Brunner, Climbing' (shell-pink). A good choice for climbing up a fruit tree in a small garden is 'New Dawn,' with pale, silvery-pink flowers that last through summer and into autumn.

Rosa *'Fritz Nobis,'* complemented here by the foliage of Berberis thunbergii *'Rose Glow,'* only flowers once, but is comparatively resistant to disease.

Annual cosmos, provided they are dead-headed regularly, look appropriate in the mixed border and are good for filling in any gaps. The tall white flowers to the right are the half-hardy annual Cleome *(spider flower). White* Buddleia davidii, *which should be pruned hard in spring, forms the background.*

Hardy perennials

The mainstay of our flower gardens, hardy herbaceous perennials form an endless pageant of flower, color and scent that changes imperceptibly day by day, as each plant in turn steps into the limelight, blooms and gradually fades, to finally retire underground for winter rest. To use these plants is perhaps the most exciting form of gardening, for despite the most elaborate plans, you never know exactly what effect you are going to achieve.

If you plant a conifer, three months later it will probably look pretty much the same. Not so the herbaceous perennial. You have to juggle so many different elements at once: height, color, flowering time, habit, foliage and, to refine the subject further and include the joker in the pack, light itself. Colors change and react differently to each other with each shift in the arc of the sun.

In the wild, clumps of herbaceous plants constantly move on into fresh territory, searching for that extra little something in their diet that is quickly used up. You will notice in a neglected border that the center of each plant has become thin and sparse of flower, while the outer shoots are plump and better nourished. So, apart from choosing a position where the plant will prosper and at the same time flatter its neighbors, a very close eye should be kept to see how well it is flowering. If it does not look as good as last year, and has become overcrowded, with congested shoots and roots, it needs dividing and replanting in fresh soil (see page 90). A comment here: in a long-established border, if you dig a special hole for a new young plant, and put in some rotted garden compost and fertilizer, the surrounding plants will be delighted too—their roots will greedily move in, elbowing out the new plant. A better plan is to dig and manure an area, say 6 ft. square, and replant, giving all the plants an equal chance.

Hardy perennial plants are extensively covered in the chapter Key Plants (see page 110).

*Love-in-a-mist (*Nigella damascena*) only has to be sown once, and from then on it will seed itself. Plants established in this way make much stronger plants than they did the first year.*

Hardy annuals

In their brief but brilliant season annuals add life and sparkle to the flower garden—last year's dramatic effect may be readily repeated and failures are quickly forgotten. In young gardens, with lots of gaps between perennials and shrubs, there is room to amuse oneself by trying out something new.

First clean the ground and dig in well-rotted garden compost, or old manure. Firm the soil by treading, and rake it level. Spread on some general fertilizer, and rake it in. You can either scatter the seed in informal drifts, or (a better method if you are unsure how to differentiate between the seedling and newly germinated weeds) make little drills about ½ in. deep, sow the seed thinly, cover with soil and firm gently. Carefully mark the area with canes. The seedlings should be thinned out in stages, to allow for further losses, according to the directions given on the packet.

Also printed on the packet are suitable months for sowing, but no mention is made of exactly what sort of condition the soil should be in. Rather like trying to describe how a perfect sponge cake should be to a novice cook, it is all a matter of texture. To sit around in cold, wet soggy soil is no inducement to a seed to sprout. Choose a nice spring day, when the sun is out to warm the soil, and wind has begun to dry the surface, so it looks lovely and crumbly: the soil is then what is known as friable. Heavy soils are improved by digging in manure, compost, coarse sand or grit, which much benefit the structure of the soil, thus assisting drainage.

After the first year some hardy annuals (given in the list on the right) will sow themselves. By so doing they seem to make much more robust, floriferous plants than they would have done the first year. Regarding annual poppies, it is easy to breed your own strain by staking the ones you particularly like. Allow these alone to ripen and drop their seed, and pull all the others out as soon as the petals fade, before they set seed.

SELF-SEEDING ANNUALS

Calendula

Consolida

Cosmos

Limnanthes

Lobularia maritima

Nigella damascena

Omphalodes linifolia

Papaver somniferum

Tropaeolum majus

Half-hardy annuals and tender perennials

Many of the plants we think of as annuals are in fact tender perennials or shrubs grown as annuals. Although they will sometimes survive a mild winter, and you will see brave young shoots on such plants as *Argyranthemum* 'Jamaica Primrose' and *A. frutescens*, *Verbena* 'Silver Anne,' *V.* 'Lawrence Johnston,' and *V.* 'Sissinghurst,' and even *Helichrysum petiolare*, unless you have a very sheltered garden you are probably better off to start afresh with young plants each year. Alternatively, you may be able to keep your plants going from year to year by taking cuttings in early autumn (see page 92) and over-wintering them in a greenhouse or conservatory.

Pelargoniums, tender *Fuchsia*, *Canna*, some *Salvia* and many more come under this heading—and these are all plants to use for that most fascinating form of instant gardening, growing plants in containers.

However, beware of putting these plants outside too soon in early summer, when there is still a danger of cold nights, or they will get such a setback that they could take weeks to recover. If you have a greenhouse or conservatory, you can gradually harden them off by day and put them back inside for the night. See page 96 for growing half-hardy annuals from seed.

Biennials

As you sow the seeds of biennial plants (those that grow one year and flower, set seed and die the second), think of all the delight you are laying down for next year. Seed of foxgloves, wallflowers, stocks, forget-me-nots, Canterbury bells, sweet Williams, honesty, for example, is sown from early summer on, in moderately rich soil, to give the plants plenty of time to build up before winter. The seedlings should be transplanted about 9 in. apart, and moved to their final position in early autumn or left until spring in cold areas.

Eryngium giganteum is a distinctive biennial, known by many people as 'Miss Willmott's Ghost.' The first year all you have is an insignificant rosette of leaves, but the following summer branching heads of bluish thistle flowers arise, which gradually pale to gleaming silver-gray. It does not transplant well and is better when it has seeded itself. To ensure continuity pull most of them out but leave a few to seed.

Bulbs

There are few places in the garden where you cannot manage to fit in a few bulbs. You can have ribbons of snowdrops and crocuses under deciduous trees; *Iris reticulata* and *I. histrioides* 'Major' and little tulips like *Tulipa linifolia* in well-drained raised beds; erythroniums and *Fritillaria pyrenaica* in shady beds; *Nerine* and *Amaryllis* in hot sunny beds beneath walls; crown imperials (*Fritillaria imperialis*), larger alliums—*Allium christophii* and *A. aflatunense*—*Galtonia*, and as many *Lilium regale* as you can possibly afford in the mixed border.

All the little blue bulbs of spring—grape hyacinths (*Muscari*), *Scilla*, *Chionodoxa* and *Puschkinia*—will make rivulets of blue among the front of the flower bed; and at the back, where their dying leaves will not show, will be daffodils. Tulips, lavishly bought, will form vivid patches of scarlet and maroon, interplanted with crimson-flushed young leaves of astilbes and peonies, while the pristine goblets of *Tulipa* 'White Triumphator' (of which you will want to buy more each year) will shine from newly emerging greens of the border.

Bulbs should be planted at roughly twice their own depth. Rich, well-drained soil is appreciated by most bulbs, but farmyard manure should be avoided except when very well rotted. Bonemeal is a good fertilizer. Most bulbs should be planted when dormant; snowdrops are one exception, they should be moved "in the green," just after flowering. Daffodils do not mind being moved just after flowering, provided you water them well, and you can at least see where you are putting them for next year.

When growing bulbs in grass, the leaves must have time to build up the bulb for next year—it is essential to wait until they are starting to go yellow and die before mowing the grass around them. Suggested daffodils for naturalizing in grass include 'February Gold,' 'February Silver,' 'Beryl,' 'Jack Snipe,' 'Jenny,' 'Jumblie,' 'Little Witch,' 'Peeping Tom,' 'Tête à Tête' and *Narcissus pseudonarcissus*.

Spring bulbs, Tulipa 'White Parrot,' white daffodils and grape hyacinths (Muscari) are seen with forget-me-nots (Myosotis) and the emerging foliage of hostas.

A sunny raised bed

This raised bed in the sun, with very well drained soil, is the ideal place in which to grow easy alpines and small, special sun-lovers. (See page 34 for making a raised bed.) The base of the low walls will provide further planting places, with varying aspects—use the shady side for *Ramonda*, *Haberlea* and ferns.

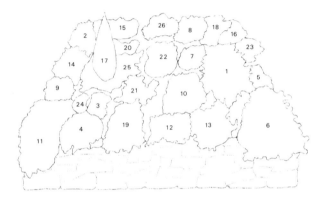

A raised bed is a good place for planting little bulbs such as *Iris reticulata*, small daffodils (*Narcissus*), *Leucojum autumnale* and hardy cyclamen, where they are much less likely to be dug up by mistake. A close eye should be kept to ensure that some of the more rampant growers (*Helianthemum*, for example) do not smother the choicer items. A good trim after flowering will help.

The bed is shown in late spring/early summer, when many alpine plants look their best.

1 *Agapanthus* 'Lilliput'
2 *Alyssum saxatile citrinum*
3 *Antennaria dioica* 'Rosea'
4 *Artemisia schmidtiana* 'Nana'
5 *Campanula cochlearifolia* 'Elizabeth Oliver'
6 *Chrysanthemopsis hosmariense*
7 *Crepis incana*
8 *Daphne cneorum*
9 *Dianthus* 'Pike's Pink'
10 *Diascia cordata*
11 *Dryas octopetala*
12 *Erodium chrysanthum*
13 *Geranium cinereum* 'Ballerina'
14 *Geranium cinereum subcaulescens*
15 *Helianthemum* 'Wisley Pink'
16 *Iberis sempervirens* 'Little Gem'
17 *Juniperus communis* 'Compressa'
18 *Linum perenne*
19 *Origanum* 'Kent Beauty'
20 *Oxalis adenophylla*
21 *Primula marginata* 'Linda Pope'
22 *Pulsatilla vulgaris*
23 *Saxifraga* 'Southside Seedling'
24 *Sempervivum arachnoideum*
25 *Thymus serpyllum*
26 *Verbascum* 'Letitia'

This raised bed is devoted to alpine subjects and small, choice herbaceous plants that enjoy full sun. A layer of gravel on top of the planting medium helps to prevent weeds' germinating, conserve summer moisture and ensure good winter drainage—an essential requirement of alpines.

CARING FOR
THE FLOWER GARDEN

Managing the garden, like running a business, is a matter of distinguishing between the essential jobs that must be done immediately, and those that can be put in the file marked "pending." With absolutely no consideration for your lifestyle, the lawn is going to continue to grow and the groundsel to release its myriad seeds. If you leave the grass too long before mowing, you will have a sickly-looking yellow mat and if you do not catch the groundsel before it seeds it will have colonized the garden for years to come. On the other hand, you can take your time over some gardening tasks, such as pruning roses.

The plants in this picture—roses, love-in-a-mist (Nigella damascena), Phaiophleps nigricans *(formerly* Sisyrinchium) *and the little, daisy-like* Erigeron karvinskianus *(in the foreground)—all have differing needs: while roses do require a certain amount of care, the* Erigeron *is a star plant for not needing any attention whatsoever.*

Essential tools

Regular garden tasks like pruning, dead-heading and tidying are done efficiently and quickly provided you have the correct tools. A wheelbarrow will enable you to transport herbaceous material to the compost heap; the kind with a wheel like a large ball is light to move, but a traditional one serves just as well for most jobs.

A spade, of a size and weight that feels right for you, is the first indispensable implement to be bought, plus a garden fork to go with it. Once you have broken a few wooden-handled spades you may decide to invest in one that is solid stainless steel. These are rather expensive and a bit heavier, but they cut like a knife through butter, are easy to keep clean and give you great confidence if you are doing a heavy job such as digging up a small tree. For many garden jobs, such as preparing planting holes, you need both spade and fork—the spade for making the initial hole, the fork for loosening the soil in the bottom of the hole and for mixing in the compost or manure. The spade is then used for refilling the hole and the fork for stirring up the surface and tidying up.

A trowel is an essential tool used for planting and for rooting out large weeds. Choose the best you can afford as cheap trowels are a poor investment—the thin metal part joining the handle to the trowel is inclined to bend at the most inconvenient moments. A stainless-steel trowel is well worth the initial expense. A small handfork has many different uses —tweaking out weeds, stirring up the surface of the soil and planting.

A good pair of hand pruners will be in use throughout the year for pruning, dead-heading, cutting back herbaceous plants in autumn and gathering flowers for the house. Here again the cheaper kinds are a waste of money; they lose their cutting edge or fall to bits too soon. Choose a pair with brightly colored handles, as shears have a habit of disappearing into bushes or hiding in compost heaps. You may also need long-handled heavy-duty pruners or loppers for cutting thicker branches.

A useful item is a tool rather like a small handfork on the end of a long stick. With this you can grub out weeds without stepping on the flower bed or, if you have left footprints, you can use it to loosen the soil. This implement is especially useful for the disabled, who cannot kneel or bend down easily.

A good watering can is one that is well balanced when full—when you carry it, you should feel that the weight is evenly distributed. You will need a coarse rose for general watering and a fine rose for watering seedlings and cuttings. A metal rose is usually more satisfactory than a plastic one. A small, extra watering can is handy for winter use under glass—you will be less inclined to overwater with it.

Other items you will require include a wheelbarrow; a stiff broom for dislodging mud from paths and a soft broom for general sweeping; a draw hoe, for scraping away small weeds and drawing out seed drills, or a Dutch hoe for breaking up the soil; shears; saw; sprayer; rake; lawn mower.

Rather than spend valuable time hunting for the trowel, tripping over the rake and scraping dried mud off the spade before starting work, make a habit of putting all your tools back, clean and dry, in the same place each time you use them.

Preparing a flower bed

Before preparing the soil, any serious weeds, such as ground elder, bindweed, quack grass and brambles, should first be sprayed with the appropriate herbicide (several times if necessary). However impatient you are to begin planting, this will save time in the long run. Any trees and shrubs you are discarding should be dug out. If you are doing this yourself you know the job will be done properly, but if you decide that this is heavy work and get somebody else in to do it, keep a close eye on what they are up to: make sure they do not take out the trunk and some of the surface roots, quickly fill in the hole and go home to tea—roots left behind can be a source of honey fungus that will spread to other shrubs and trees. If you have inherited only annual weeds, chickweed, groundsel, shepherd's purse and so on, they can be dug in as you go along (see page 87). Carefully dig out perennial weeds, such as nettles, dandelions, docks and buttercups.

Ideally, you should dig a flower bed in autumn, so that frost can break up the clods of earth you have thrown up. By the spring, these will have broken down to a fine tillage. Take care not to mix any subsoil at the bottom of the trenches in with the topsoil. The subsoil is a different color from the topsoil, which makes it easy to recognize.

Burning bush (Dictamnus albus) in the center must never be transplanted, so place it correctly the first time, in well-prepared soil. Its white flowers are echoed by the iris in the foreground and the variegated foliage of the Euonymus fortunei (left).

How to dig a flower bed

Using the spade, first dig a trench, about 2 ft. wide, and barrow the soil up to the far end of the area you are about to dig. Next, break up the soil with a fork in the bottom of the trench you have just excavated. Then fork in well-rotted manure or compost and spread it about. You then dig another trench alongside, using the excavated soil to fill up the first trench. Continue like this. When you get to the last trench, fill it in with the soil you barrowed up there. This operation is called single digging.

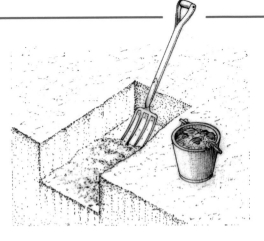

Add about a 1-gallon bucketful of manure per square yard, from a barrow.

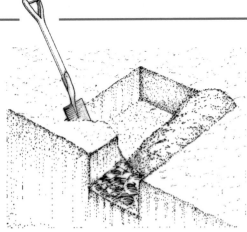

Fill up each trench as you go with soil excavated from the new trench.

Planting

Mid-autumn is a good time for planting hardy perennials, when the soil is still warm. Any plants that you suspect may be tender in your area, as well as silver-leaved plants in general and grasses in particular, are better left till spring. Evergreen shrubs also establish best in spring, when the growing season is starting in earnest and their roots grow rapidly as the soil warms up. Try and choose a time when the soil is neither too wet nor too dry.

If you are planting a newly dug and prepared bed, add only a light dressing of fertilizer (either a balanced fertilizer or bonemeal) as you plant. But for planting in an existing flower bed you will need to be more generous. Work whatever would benefit the plant into the bottom of the planting hole: extra grit to lighten heavy soil, plenty of well-rotted compost, manure or leaf mold to enrich all soils and enable the roots to grow easily through it, plus bonemeal and general fertilizer.

Make certain that the plant's rootball is thoroughly moist before planting. If the rootball seems dry, give it a good soaking for an hour or two beforehand. Bare-rooted plants can be soaked in a bucket or a water barrel. Never expose roots to hot sun or drying winds. If the roots are tightly wound around each other, unravel some of them gently.

Always make a planting hole much bigger than the plant's container. Even for a herbaceous perennial in, say, a 6 in. pot, you should prepare a hole 1½ ft. in diameter, 1–1½ ft. deep.

For planting a tree or large shrub, using a spade, dig a hole 3 ft. or more in diameter. Place the top layer of soil to one side, then break up the next layer of soil with the spade or fork; you may need to use a pickaxe if the subsoil is hard. Work in two to three bucketfuls of bulky organic matter (well-rotted manure or compost). Replace some topsoil and work in bonemeal and general fertilizer.

Always water well after planting, even if it is raining. Keep an eye on newly planted plants: young trees and shrubs benefit from being mulched immediately after watering. Use two cans of water per plant and cover the moist area with a loose layer of organic material about 4 in. deep—old manure, bark chippings or compost. This prevents evaporation and will rot down and enrich the soil.

Bedding plants do not need soil that is very rich in nutrients since this will only encourage lush growth at the expense of flowers. If the soil is in good condition, it should only be necessary to give a sprinkling of general fertilizer. Use the trowel for planting and water through a fine rose.

Refilling the planting hole

Refill the hole around the new plant's roots with topsoil, checking that you have the correct level. It is important to plant at the same soil level the plant was originally growing. Peonies, for example, if planted too deeply, will fail to flower and, at worst, will rot. If trees and shrubs are planted too deeply, the extra soil around the base of the plant will rot the bark and ultimately kill the plant. Firm the soil around the roots.

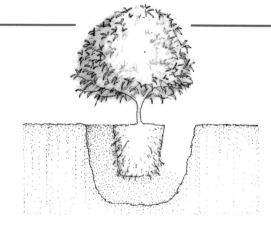

Tread with your feet to firm the soil around newly planted trees and shrubs.

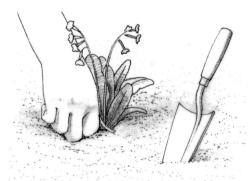

Firm in small plants with gentle pressure from your hands. Give the plant a little tug to test that it is securely planted.

Watering

As more areas become subject to water restrictions, yet more gardeners have to find out how drought-tolerant a plant is. And (as previously mentioned on page 16) it is good husbandry to put those plants that are going to need extra watering—*Astilbe*, *Rodgersia*, *Gentiana asclepiadea* (willow gentian), for example—in the same area, so that you are not rushing hither and thither with cans of water.

Your plants should be encouraged to be self-sufficient, to reach out their roots far and wide in search of water—a good root system, spread out over a large area, will serve them well in times of drought. If you are going to water plants in the open ground, give them a generous amount, that is, about 4 gallons per square yard, and aim the can at the base of the plant. Too little water (just a sprinkle here and there on the foliage) simply encourages the roots toward the surface of the soil, giving them little support for drier weather.

It is sometimes said that you should not water in strong sunshine, because water droplets act as lenses and may cause foliage to scorch, but if you have a lot of garden to cover you may decide that it is better to scorch the odd leaf rather than see your plants suffer. But there is the problem of fast evaporation if you water in sunshine, so ideally you should water in the evening, making good use of available water and giving plants a chance to recover during the night.

Be especially careful over watering under glass. In winter, growth is at a standstill and the plants cannot absorb excess water. If you splash water about, you are also giving an open invitation to gray mold (*Botrytis*), a fungus that thrives on close, damp conditions. An overwatered plant has a sad, limp look about it, the pot feels too heavy and the soil cold and sodden; your only recourse is to stop watering and hope the roots gradually renew themselves. A guide to winter watering is "when in doubt, don't."

In summer you should have quite a different attitude: the temperature under glass can rise alarmingly fast when the sun comes out. Even in spring if you go out for the day and forget to open the ventilation, you could come home to find trays of

young seedlings shriveled up. Your plants will need a thorough watering every day.

The watering of containers demands particular attention. It is easy to ignore pots in winter, thinking that there has been plenty of rain, and totally forgetting about how drying winds can be. Well-established evergreens, in particular, may have formed an umbrella of foliage over their pots, so rain cannot penetrate to their roots. Once or twice a week during winter, check over your containers and give them a good soaking if necessary. A *Camellia* in a large tub, for example, would need 1 gallon of water per watering. However, do not water in frosty weather. In summer, containers demand an immense amount of water, and may need watering twice a day in very hot weather.

Rodgersia pinnata 'Superba,' Dactylorhiza braunii *and* Brunnera macrophylla 'Dawson's White' *are three plants which like the ground nicely moist at all times.*

Feeding your plants

In order to grow flowers well, the first essential is to look after your soil. Whatever your soil, be it light sandy or heavy clay, the secret of improving it is the addition of decayed organic matter rich in humus. Curiously enough, decayed organic matter is highly beneficial to diametrically opposed types of soil: to a thin, sandy soil it will act like a sponge and make it much more moisture-retentive, while it will lighten, warm and help break up a soil of heavy clay. It will greatly improve the structure of both, so that the multitude of plant roots, on their busy search for water and plant nutrients, can move easily through the soil.

The garden store cupboard

No amount of later cultivation will take the place of initial thorough digging and preparation of the soil with the liberal addition of compost or well-rotted manure (see page 81). But with a well-stocked garden store cupboard you can offer your plants generous helpings of whatever they need when planting, feeding or top-dressing them. Compost, manure or leaf mold—individually or in any combination—can be mixed with the soil in the bottom of planting holes (using, say, half to one bucketful per herbaceous plant and two to four bucketfuls or more for a tree or shrub).

The compost heap The nerve center of the garden, the compost heap is a wonderful source of organic matter rich in humus. The breaking down of all your garden trash and vegetable trimmings from the kitchen within a well-made compost heap converts them into a dark, crumbly substance, with a sweet and settled smell. When vegetable matter decomposes it heats up, thus encouraging all sorts of bacteria and microscopic fungi to multiply at a fast rate, and get on with their business of transforming the waste into compost. Grass mowings and green, leafy weeds heat up quickly, while woody stems of herbaceous plants are much slower. The idea is to achieve a balance between the two, using the coarser material, chopped up herbaceous stems and so on,

interspersed with softer, leafy matter. Too thick a layer of grass mowings, for example, will turn into a slimy mess and too thick a layer of woody material might not heat up properly. Soil, attached to weeds and discarded plants, and path sweepings all go into the mixture. You can use a brand-name compost activator (more likely to be necessary in autumn and winter) or cover each 10 in. layer of refuse with a thin layer of fresh farmyard manure. The finished heap should be capped with a 1 in. layer of soil and a sheet of polyethylene for insulation. Do not put on autumn leaves (these are better kept separately to make leaf mold, as they are slow to rot down), or grass cuttings when you have just used a lawn herbicide, or material like chicken bones from the kitchen—there is nothing a mother rat likes more than a nice warm compost heap.

Making compost Ideally, you should have two compost bins side by side, made out of slatted wood, and about 4 ft. square. The slats on the front of each bin should be removable to allow access. As the first becomes full up, you can turn the heap into the second bin, an action which further aids the rotting process. Compost bins can also be made out of bricks or concrete blocks, leaving plenty of gaps for aeration. Brand-name plastic compost bins with holes in the sides are good for small gardens.

Mature compost is welcomed by just about any plant, with very few exceptions, one of these being New Zealand native plants, which resent rich feeding. It may be used for the initial digging, for working into the bottom of planting holes, for mulching and, when well matured, small quantities may be required in potting mixtures. If you garden on limy soil, be wary about using garden compost for acid-loving plants, since it might contain some lime, introduced by weeds with garden soil on their roots.

Farmyard manure Thoroughly rotted farmyard manure is one of the best sorts of nourishment for the soil. It is worth every effort to locate, but never refuse a fresh load—just store the heap for a few

Erythronium revolutum

One of the most enchanting early spring bulbs for the flower garden, if you start off with just one or two, they will soon seed themselves to build up a colony. From western North America, E. revolutum is a variable species with flowers ranging from pale to deep pink, and the leaves may be lightly marbled in gray-green or heavily mottled in chocolate. They do not like being dried out at any stage, even when dormant, so choose a position in part-shade in well-drained, humus-rich and moisture-retentive soil. Mark their position well, mulch annually with leaf mold and propagate by division, replanting immediately, soon after flowering.

months until it matures, under a sheet of polyethylene to prevent the goodness leaching away. It can be used during the initial digging, and for preparing the planting holes of any plants, especially roses, delphiniums, peonies, dahlias and clematis.

Leaf mold Leaf mold is the flaky, brown, crumbly material found in woods, just under the layer of leaves that fell the previous autumn. You can make leaf mold from your own autumn leaves by simply stacking them in a wire-netting enclosure; the best leaf mold comes from oak and beech leaves. Never put in plane or sycamore leaves, as they take too long to rot, or leathery evergreens like yew or holly. Pine needles should also be avoided as they take too long to decay and the resulting mold is too acid. Rich in humus, leaf mold is the perfect soil-enricher for woodland plants; it can be worked in as you plant or used as a mulch. If it is in short supply, save it for putting beneath your trilliums and snowdrops.

Leaf mold is also one of the ingredients in a general potting mixture for alpines (one-third each of leaf mold, loam and sharp grit). For use in potting mixtures it should crumble up nicely when rubbed between your hands, or it can be rubbed through a coarse garden sieve. As a mulch it can be used as it is.

General fertilizer While the importance of adding organic matter to your soil cannot be overemphasized, your plants are going to need an extra tonic in the form of a general fertilizer. This contains a balanced combination of nitrogen, phosphorus and potassium, three vital elements for healthy plant growth. Broadly speaking, nitrogen builds up leafy tissue—the leaves, stems and shoots—phosphorus encourages root growth and potassium develops the flowers and fruit. On a packet of fertilizer these are indicated as N, P and K, respectively.

A general fertilizer is used when planting and can be applied to the flower beds in spring, working it in lightly with a fork; it can also be scattered around any plant that does not seem to be doing well. Never exceed the amount recommended on the package.

Bonemeal Made from ground-up bones, bonemeal is a slow-acting fertilizer. Applied in autumn or spring, it is excellent for putting in the bottom of the planting hole for trees, shrubs, roses, bulbs and herbaceous plants. Coarsely ground bonemeal is particularly useful for bulbs, which in general dislike farmyard manure or bulky organic matter, and should be either added when planting them or mixed into the surrounding soil as they appear in spring. It can be applied at up to 8 oz. per square yard. Finely ground bonemeal (apply at 3–4 oz. per square yard) is faster-acting.

Liquid fertilizer and foliar feeds Liquid fertilizers and foliar feeds are good, fast pick-me-ups for use on plants during summer, particularly for plants in containers, where there is a restricted root run, and for those in soil-less potting composts, where plant foods are rapidly used up.

Sand and grit There is no food value in sand, but it is essential for assisting drainage either in the open ground or as a constituent of potting composts and cutting mixtures. On no account should builder's sand be used. Sharp sand is clean and free of silt: when you scrunch it in your hand it should feel sharp. It is also useful for putting around bulbs such as crown imperials (*Fritillaria imperialis*) and lilies to stop waterlogging and to deter slugs.

Grit comprises little chippings of stone which should feel sharp when you take a handful. It is invaluable for working into heavy soil to lighten it and assist drainage, and as a constituent of potting composts for alpines and bulbs, as well as for adding to the soil when making a raised bed (see page 34).

Mulching Rotted compost, manure and leaf mold all make ideal material for mulching, as do bark chippings. A layer of any of these, about 4 in. deep, applied in spring or autumn when the soil is damp but not cold, is an excellent way both of keeping weeds from germinating and of conserving moisture around the plants' roots (see page 82).

Dead-heading

Pansies (Viola) should be regularly dead-headed (preferably every day) throughout the summer to prevent them setting seed and to ensure a long flowering display. They are planted here with scabious (Scabiosa caucasica) and Stachys byzantina.

third strong-looking leaf below the dead flower—a new shoot will form at this point. It is tempting to dead-head dahlias by the nipping-off-flower-head method, but you end up with a lot of unsightly stalks. Cut off the faded bloom and stalk together, just above a leaf. If you remove the crumpled bells of *Campanula persicifolia*, new ones will form and you can even convince a columbine (*Aquilegia*) that it should produce more flowers by frustrating its attempts to set seed. There are many other plants that will not only bloom for much longer, but also look prettier while they are doing it, that deserve the small effort dead-heading requires. But spare the pruning shears with plants that have a second season of beauty with their seed heads (listed opposite).

In some cases the reason for dead-heading is to prevent the plant from wasting its energies producing unwanted seed. Young *Rhododendron*, lilacs and other flowering shrubs benefit from having their green, newly formed seed heads removed, and bulbs and corms (unless you want them to seed themselves) should be using their strength for building up next year's storage organ, so pinch off the old flower at the top of the flower stem.

Weeding

There is no better way of keeping in touch with your plants than by hand weeding—you would miss so much if somebody else did it for you. By working near the plants you are instantly reminded of their needs: you might see a plant that needs urgent division as it has become overcrowded, another that is fainting from lack of water or yet another that the slugs are starting to attack. And, when you have finished the bed, comes the best part of all: standing in the sun, doing nothing in particular, lost in admiration of a weed-free bed.

With weeding, as with many other gardening jobs, timing is most important. Put it off for a week or two, and you have double the work to do. Weeds are brilliantly adapted to survival: thistles, dandelions and groundsel send their offspring off on

Dead-heading means more than drifting around the garden with a basket, the pruning shears and a dreamy air. Most plants have one specific aim in life, to flower and form seed: as soon as their seeds are ripe, perennials retire for the year while annuals and biennials, their life-cycle complete, will shortly die. But we gardeners have other plans for them—we would like them to decorate our gardens by flowering for the longest possible time. By removing their faded flower-heads, many plants are persuaded to make valiant efforts to produce yet more flowers.

If you want to keep up the display of roses (except the old-fashioned kinds that only flower once, or those species and cultivars that produce good hips), they must be dead-headed. Cut the dead flowers off neatly with pruning shears just above the second or parachutes to new ground; ground elder and bind-weed establish colonies beneath the soil; shepherd's purse and annual meadow grass are adept at ripening and shedding their seed in a matter of days, even in winter. There are also those "weeds" that we ourselves introduce to the garden, such as the Welsh poppy or the white form of the rosebay willow herb, which are as dangerous in behavior as they are beautiful to behold.

To keep control of these masters of survival, you have to work systematically through a bed, when it is due for weeding, and try to get it all done in one session. Dig out deep-rooted weeds like a dandelion properly, making sure its flower-heads do not seed.

There are two seasons of the year when it is vital to be in control. The first is early in spring, when small weeds are busy concealing themselves beneath bulb foliage and the expanding leaves of herbaceous plants. You have to be specially vigilant at this time, or they will have shed their seed unnoticed. The second time of year is on the cusp between spring and summer, when there is a great surge of growth. The cleaner you get your flower beds at this time, the less work you will have later in summer. As soon as this hard work is done, choose a time when the soil is thoroughly moist and spread a thick mulch about

4 in. deep (see page 85) around the plants, smothering weed seeds intent on germination.

Methods of weeding vary: a hoe or a small fork on a long or short handle (see page 80) is useful, but never use a hoe near surface-rooting plants, such as heathers and *Rhododendron*—you could seriously damage the roots. When there is hot, drying sun the weeds will shrivel fast, so they can be left on the surface of the soil. But when weeding in cooler weather, make sure the weeds get properly buried, or pick them out by hand. Some people walk all over the bed, taking out weeds with a trowel and putting them in a bucket; they then go back and loosen the compacted soil with a garden fork.

Weeds with long taproots like dandelions and docks, that are growing in awkward places, can be dealt with by painting the leaves with an appropriate selective herbicide. Bindweed stems and leaves can be dipped into a jar of a systemic herbicide.

Have the greatest respect for all garden chemicals; apply them with care as a misdirected splash could kill a nearby plant. Keep all products safely out of reach of children and pets and have separate equipment for use only with chemicals. Always follow the instructions with care, wear rubber gloves and wash your hands and all equipment afterward.

PLANTS WITH ATTRACTIVE SEEDHEADS

Allium
Clematis
Dierama
Dipsacus
Iris foetidissima
Lunaria
Nigella damascena
Papaver
Pennisetum
Phlomis
Physalis
Stipa gigantea

Five common weeds

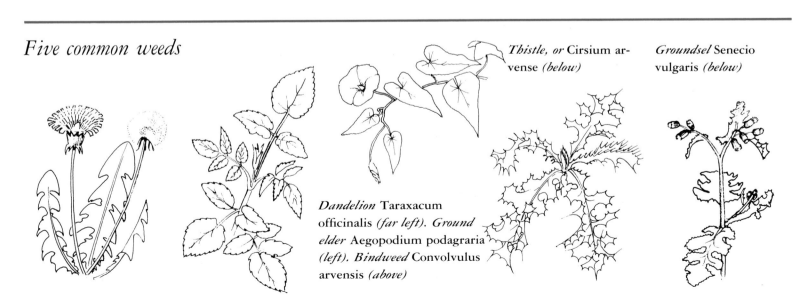

Thistle, or Cirsium arvense *(below)*

Groundsel Senecio vulgaris *(below)*

Dandelion Taraxacum officinalis *(far left). Ground elder* Aegopodium podagraria *(left). Bindweed* Convolvulus arvensis *(above)*

Pruning

Those new to gardening are sometimes convinced that regular pruning is as essential to the health of a shrub as are food and water. However, most shrubs will grow, flower and fruit, with never a cut in sight. The primary reason for pruning is to keep a plant vigorous, healthy, well balanced and in scale with the garden, as well as to encourage it to flower or fruit well. Therefore, a sound general rule is to take out any dead, damaged or diseased, and weak wood, which will only use up the plant's energy to no purpose. Shrubs that flower on the previous season's wood, such as *Deutzia*, *Philadelphus*, *Weigela* and *Buddleia alternifolia*, should have some of the weaker shoots, which have just flowered, taken out immediately after blooming is finished. This gives the new shoots room to grow, and the longest time to develop and ripen for the next year's display. Early-flowering shrubs in this group, such as *Jasminum nudiflorum* and *Forsythia*, should also have their flowering shoots pruned as soon as the blossom fades.

Shrubs that flower on the current season's wood, blooming from mid-summer onward, such as *Buddleia davidii* cultivars, *Ceanothus × delileanus* 'Gloire de Versailles,' *Caryopteris × clandonensis* and *Hydrangea paniculata* cultivars, must be pruned hard in early spring to allow flowering shoots to grow.

Pruning roses

All roses, without exception, should be pruned hard, without fail, immediately after planting, to encourage strong young shoots from the base. Annual pruning is done in mid-spring, at a time when winter is well over, before the roses waste their effort in a burst of spring growth. The aim is to keep the center of the bush open to light and air; take out all dead and weak wood and remove any crossing branches as they may cause damage by chafing.

By making the pruning cut just above an outward-pointing bud, you are encouraging the plant to send out a new shoot which will grow away from the center of the plant, thus avoiding a congested tangle of branches in the middle. Make the cut about ¼ in. above the bud; it should slope downward away from the bud, at 45 degrees, so that rain runs off easily and rot does not set in.

Large and cluster-flowered roses

Also known as hybrid teas and floribundas respectively, these should be clipped over in late autumn, to prevent them rocking in the wind. In spring, large-flowered roses should have each shoot pruned again by about half, and cluster-flowered by about a third.

Pruning roses

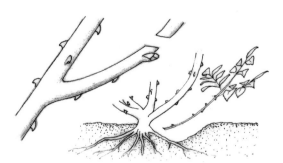

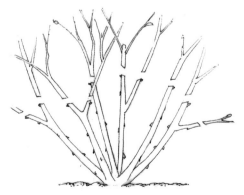

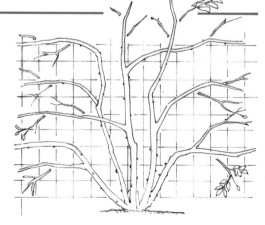

With all roses, make the pruning cut above an outward-facing bud. Carefully pull off any suckers at below ground level.

Large-flowered and cluster-flowered roses should have a third of their branches pruned back in the autumn to stop wind-rock.

In spring, prune the side-shoots of climbers by two-thirds; leave the main stems alone.

will find some pieces with a woody stem 8 in. long, and no roots; if you plant these stems firmly, up to the leaf rosette, they will soon make roots. When replanting, fork in some well-rotted manure or compost, at a rate of roughly two bucketfuls per square yard, then sprinkle on bonemeal, a general fertilizer, or both, and work this in with the fork.

When to divide

In the heyday of the herbaceous border, when there was plenty of labor, every three years or so all the plants would be lifted at once, the border would be double-dug and manured (see page 81), and the divided plants replanted. Even in a smaller border this is a major undertaking. So every year, check over your plants, and decide which of them need division, and deal with them one at a time. Signs of being in need of division, apart from the center of the plant becoming old and woody, are fewer and smaller flowers and an overall appearance of lack of vigor. On rich, retentive soil, plants will continue to flourish for longer than on thin, well-drained soils. On poor soils Michaelmas daisies, *Phlox*, *Helenium*, *Astilbe*, *Rudbeckia*, *Leucanthemum × superbum* and all the general run of herbaceous plants will need dividing every three years, but you may have another year's

grace on better soil. Rather than plant a whole bed, it is better to re-do a small section, say 6–10 ft. square, at one time by lifting the plants, digging that part of the border, adding some organic matter and replanting. This enables you to replenish the soil and will allow divisions of different herbaceous plants to compete with established plants.

Some plants—*Hosta*, *Veratrum*, day lilies (*Hemerocallis*), peonies (*Paeonia*), *Kirengeshoma*, Oriental poppies (*Papaver orientale*) and hellebores (*Helleborus*), for example—can remain *in situ* for many years. If you want another plant of any one of these, just cut off a segment without disturbing the parent plant. But hellebores and hostas eventually start to deteriorate. The best method of dealing with this is to dig up the plant in early spring—after flowering in the case of hellebores, but with hostas when the shoots are starting to form—and wash all the soil off the roots. Using a sharp knife, cut the plant into sections, making sure each piece has a shoot, and cut away completely the woody centers and massed old root. Hellebores establish well from small divisions.

Certain herbaceous plants—*Baptisia*, *Gentiana lutea*, *Dictamnus albus*, *Gentiana asclepiadea*, for example—should never be disturbed in any way, and must be propagated from seed.

Cypripedium reginae
The queen of lady's slipper orchids, this species was cultivated by Philip Miller at the Chelsea Physic Garden and first grown at the Royal Garden, Kew, in 1770. It is a fully hardy, deciduous, terrestrial orchid, native to the northeastern United States. Flowering in early summer, the petals are white but the inflated pouch below, large enough for a bee to get lost inside, is blushed the most delicious rose-pink.

Replanting the divisions

Discard any old woody bits from the center of the plant, spread out the sections on the soil surface, spacing them roughly 1 ft. apart. (If the weather is warm, keep the divisions in a bucket of water or under a damp sack until the last minute.)

Replant the pieces at the same soil level at which the parent plant was growing. Even if it is raining, water well to settle the roots. Prick over the soil surface lightly with a fork. If you have to plant when the soil is very dry, fill up the planting hole with water first.

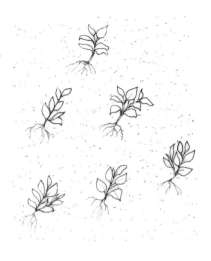

Replant the small pieces in a group, then water thoroughly.

When the soil is dry, "puddle" the plants in; fill holes with water first.

Cuttings

A cutting is a portion of stem, root or even a leaf of a plant, without roots, which, given the right conditions, will send out roots and form a new plant. An "Irishman's cutting" denotes a shoot that has a little piece of root already attached. In Ireland, cuttings are often called "slips."

Many plants—shrubs and tender perennials in particular—root easily in late summer and early autumn. At this time of year there is sufficient warmth in the sun to encourage the cuttings to form roots, but it is not so hot that they wilt too often, eventually give up and die. While these plants will still root in mid-autumn and even later, their root formation becomes slower as winter advances.

Cuttings compost

Peat has been widely used in horticulture for several decades. While its use is no longer universally acceptable, there is no doubt that peat, mixed with horticultural sand, makes a suitable compost for rooting cuttings. In areas where peat is still harvested at a sustainable level—that is, in a quantity equal to the rate of natural renewal—you can mix up your own cuttings compost using two parts of moist peat to one part of sharp sand. Research into different peat substitutes is still underway and various multipurpose composts on the market are recommended as suitable for rooting cuttings. In this section, the term "cuttings compost" means either a brand-name compost specially formulated for cuttings or your homemade peat and sand mix.

Rooting the cuttings

What you do with your cuttings depends on your general gardening arrangements. You can use either a heated propagator, a shaded cold frame with the lights closed, or an old-fashioned glass jar in the corner of a greenhouse: all prevent the cuttings from losing moisture long enough for them to form roots. The cuttings should be kept in a warm place, out of direct sun. Keep a hand sprayer full of water nearby and mist over their foliage on hot days. You can also make a sort of mini-greenhouse by placing a small stick in the middle of the pot, putting the whole thing in a polyethylene bag and tying the mouth of the bag tightly to the stick.

As soon as you think the cuttings are rooted (you will see signs of new growth or roots coming through the holes in the bottom of the pot), you can gradually give them more air. You can then pot them individually into small pots and keep them in a frost-free greenhouse for the winter.

Some of the plants in the list will only survive outdoors in mild climates. By taking cuttings and keeping them under glass for the winter you will have fine plants the following spring. Silver-leaved

Taking a stem cutting

Choose a healthy shoot about 3–4 in. long; it should be neither too old nor too young, and preferably of fairly young wood with a little heel of older wood where it was pulled off the main stem—plump little non-flowering sideshoots are ideal. Remove one or two pairs of leaves from the base of the stalk and insert the cuttings in the prepared compost, around the edge of the pot. The reason for using the edge rather than the middle is that drainage is likely to be best at that point.

Pull off a non-flowering shoot from the main stem, with a "heel."

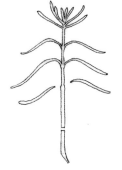

Take off the lower leaves and trim the base of the shoot if it is ragged.

Firm in the cuttings, about 1 ½ in. deep, around the edge of a pot.

plants, Mediterranean plants in general and *Pelargonium* are some of those whose cuttings do not like the enclosed, humid conditions of a propagator or polyethylene bag and prefer the shady part of a greenhouse or kitchen windowsill, out of full sun.

Stem cuttings

In late summer or early autumn choose a healthy-looking shoot as described below. With many of the plants listed (right), it should be possible to find a suitable cutting with a heel, but if you cannot find a suitable "heeled" cutting, trim your chosen piece of stem immediately below a pair of leaves. Try and find a leafy shoot with no flowers—or, if there are any flower buds, cut them off, as they will only attract mold and use up the strength of the cutting.

As soon as a cutting is removed from a plant, its first inclination is to wilt, so put it straight into a polyethylene bag until you are ready to deal with it. Remove one or two pairs of leaves from the bottom of the stalk. If, from where you pulled off the cutting from the parent plant, the heel of older wood has a straggly piece of tissue attached, trim it off cleanly with a sharp knife. Fill a 3½ in. pot with cuttings compost (see page 92)—you are not being kind by using a larger pot, only encouraging the second inclination of the cutting, which is to rot at the base. Insert the cuttings (about six per pot) firmly around the edge. Water, using a fine rose on the watering

can so as not to flood the pot.

Root cuttings

This method may be used for many herbaceous plants, including *Anchusa*, *Eryngium*, *Echinops*, *Romneya*, *Verbascum*, *Phlox*, *Papaver orientale*, *Limonium*, *Primula denticulata* and *Crambe*. The cuttings are usually taken in late winter. Dig away the soil to get at the roots. You can then cut thick roots into sections, with a straight cut at the top and a sloping cut at the bottom (this is to remind you to insert it the correct way up). Insert the cuttings vertically in a pot of cuttings compost (see page 92) and place them in a cold frame or greenhouse. Smaller roots, of plants such as *Phlox*, are placed horizontally on the surface of the compost and covered with sand.

Leaf cuttings

This method is not much used in the flower garden except for increasing *Ramonda* and *Haberlea*. Take a healthy leaf (not one of the damaged outer ones) with its leaf stalk still attached, from near the center of the plant, around mid-summer. At the base of the leaf stalk you should see the faintest sign of a bud—it is this that will form the new plant. Insert the cuttings firmly in a pot of cuttings compost (see page 92), then water and place in a shaded cold frame. Do not disturb until the following spring, when you should see nice little plants forming at the base of each leaf.

PLANTS THAT ROOT EASILY FROM CUTTINGS IN LATE SUMMER

Shrubs
Abutilon
Artemisia 'Powis Castle'
Cistus
Fuchsia
Hebe
Hedera
Hydrangea
Lavatera
Lavandula
Penstemon
Phygelius
Rosmarinus
Salvia officinalis

Herbaceous plants
Anthemis
Malva 'Primley Blue'

Tender bedding plants
Argyranthemum
Felicia
Helichrysum petiolare
Osteospermum
Pelargonium
Salvia (tender species)
Verbena

Other cuttings

Root cuttings:
During the dormant season, dig up large, fleshy roots of suitable herbaceous plants and divide them into sections 3–4 in. long, cutting the lower end at a slant. Plant the cuttings one to a pot, with the slanting end downward.

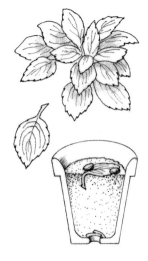

Leaf cuttings (left): Remove a well-developed leaf and lay it flat with its leaf stalk (petiole) firmly embedded in the compost. Weigh it down with small stones.
Softwood cuttings (right): Take soft, young tip cuttings in spring and strip off the lower leaves. Insert into a cuttings compost around the edge of a pot.

Softwood cuttings

Short, basal or tip cuttings of the young growing shoots of many herbaceous plants (such as *Delphinium*, cultivars of *Gentiana asclepiadea*, *Lythrum*, *Nepeta* and *Sedum*) can be taken in spring. *Dendranthema* (once called *Chrysanthemum*) are usually propagated this way, but the hardy pompons such as 'Mei-kyo' can also be propagated by division. The soft shoots are inserted around the edge of an 3 in. pot of cuttings compost (see page 92). Water and place the pot in a cold frame or cool greenhouse. New shoots of *Fuchsia* root well in spring in warmth.

Hardwood cuttings

In the flower garden this is a useful method of propagating roses. In mid-autumn, take 9–12 in. long cuttings of firm, healthy wood, with a heel; remove the leaves. In a sheltered part of the garden insert the cuttings in a small trench with some sharp sand in the bottom. Make them very firm and do not disturb them for a year. Rose cuttings can also be rooted in warmth in summer, using young shoots about 4 in. long. Often the only way to obtain some beautiful but nameless rose is by rooting it from a cutting, and roses grown this way, on their own roots, will never trouble you with suckers. Most make good plants propagated by this method, but large-flowered and cluster-flowered roses are best bought as budded plants.

Cuttings outside

Some plants root easily in the open garden. Violas such as *Viola cornuta* can be divided but some of the cultivars, for example, *Viola* 'Irish Molly' and *Viola* 'Jackanapes,' need to be propagated from cuttings. Choose a light position, but out of the sun. Make a little trench about 6 in. deep with a trowel, fill it up with cuttings compost (see page 92) and firm it well before making any holes.

Choose 2 in. chubby young non-flowering shoots from the center of the plant (the straggly, long flowering shoots will not root). Pull them off with a little tug, rather than cutting them. If the cuttings are too long, trim them to below a pair of leaves. Take off one or two pairs of the lower leaves of the cutting, being careful not to tear the stem. Make a hole in the cuttings mixture and, being careful that the base of each cutting is fully in contact with the bottom of the hole, insert the cuttings in a row. They will be in intensive care for the next week or two: this means that you should give them a sprinkle of water from the can several times on warm days. Violas are hardy and can stay where they are until the following spring.

Cuttings of pinks (*Dianthus*) dislike too-warm conditions for rooting, and also prefer being outside. In summer, select non-flowering side-shoots, known as pipings, about 3 in. long and treat them in exactly the same way.

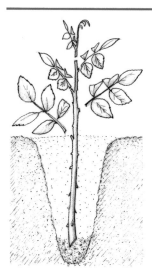

Hardwood cuttings: To propagate roses, take 9–12 in. "heeled" cuttings of mature wood from the central portion of the stem; they should be of pencil thickness. Trim off the top and strip off all their leaves. Insert them in a V-shaped trench outdoors up to at least half their length, and firm them in.

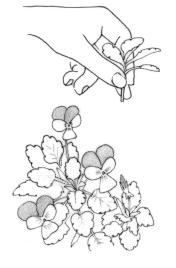

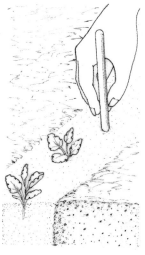

Rooting cuttings outdoors: In early autumn, pull off short, healthy non-flowering shoots from the center of a plant and remove the lower leaves. Insert them in a row into a shallow trench of specially prepared compost, making holes with a dibble or pencil. Firm them in well. Water thoroughly.

Layering

It is well worth experimenting with layering as a method of propagation, especially for plants that are expensive to buy or difficult to find, and those that you have found hard to root from cuttings. Layering happens naturally with some plants, such as *Hydrangea anomala petiolaris* and *Jasminum nudiflorum*, when the stems that come in contact with the soil form their own roots while attached to the parent plant.

Border carnations are usually propagated by this method. In high summer, when they have just finished flowering, choose a healthy, non-flowering shoot. Without removing it from the parent plant, strip off its lower pairs of leaves, leaving a tuft of foliage at the end of the shoot. Using a sharp knife, make a thin slicing cut 1 in. or so long, from the bump in the stem where the last pair of leaves were removed up to just below the remaining tuft of leaves. This should result in a slender tongue of stem that opens away from the parent plant. Work some sharp sand into a small hole in the appropriate position and lower the shoot down into it, with the cut kept open. (By encouraging the shoot tip into a vertical position, the cut should open.) Peg it firmly in with a U-shaped piece of bent wire, leaving the tuft of leaves exposed above the soil surface. Top off with the mixture, and water thoroughly. In about two months the layered shoot should have rooted.

Magnolia, *Carpenteria californica*, *Rhododendron* and choice members of the Ericaceae such as *Kalmia* and *Menziesia* may also be propagated this way. Choose a vigorous shoot near ground level and pull it gently toward the soil. Work out where the middle of the buried portion is going to come and then wound the bark at that part, by removing with a sharp knife a thin piece of bark about 1 in. long. Make a small hole about 4 in. deep and work some horticultural sand into the soil at the bottom of the hole. Peg the shoot firmly into the sandy mixture with a U-shaped piece of bent wire, and fill up the hole with the sand and soil mixture. It may be necessary to stake the shoot tip, to keep it vertical. (Do not use a multipurpose compost for layering these plants, since it may contain lime.)

Layering is also a useful way of propagating heathers. In spring, bend down some of the outer stems of the plant into the soil, so only the tips of the shoots are showing, and hold them down with a stone or piece of bent wire. The following spring the young plants may be separated from the parent and transplanted. *Daphne cneorum*, a lovely prostrate plant, with fragrant rose-pink flowers, is another ideal subject for layering. Simply mound up the stems of the plant with horticultural sand, working it down between the branches in spring. By early autumn some of the stems will have taken root and may be planted elsewhere.

Layering border carnations

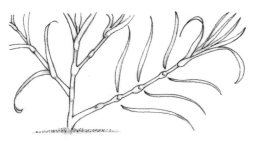

Just after flowering, remove the lower leaves from a young, healthy shoot, leaving the tuft of leaves at the end.

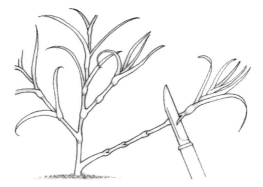

Make a 1 in. long incision along the stem with a sharp knife, just below a node; this will open away from the parent plant.

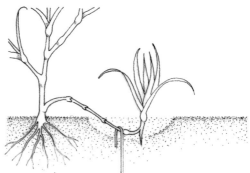

Bend the stem at this point and anchor it with bent wire into a layer of prepared compost. Water thoroughly.

Growing from seed

One great advantage of growing your own summer bedding plants is that you can pick and choose exactly what varieties you want, and can select individual colors rather than the usual mixed assortment that is available from garden centers.

Sowing half-hardy annuals

Sow the seeds in a pot or tray as described below, and leave it in a warm place. Keep a close eye on it, and wipe away surplus moisture from the pane of glass. From the moment the seeds germinate, uncover the glass, as they will need good light as well as warmth.

As soon as the seedlings have their first pair of true leaves (in addition to their first "seedling leaves") and are large enough to handle, prick them out into trays, spaced about 2 in. apart, or in individual pots for larger plants such as *Cobaea*. Hold them only by the seedling leaves—if you squeeze this too hard the plant will recover, but once the stem is damaged, that is the end of the seedling.

Careful hardening off is essential, that is to say the seedlings have to be gradually weaned from the warm, draft-free conditions in which they have been raised until they are strong enough to withstand the more rigorous conditions outdoors. If hardening off is rushed, the seedlings may get a severe check in growth, which could set them back considerably, or even kill them. Their first change in temperature might be from a heated propagator to the greenhouse proper. After a week or so here to gain strength, they can be moved to the most well-ventilated part of the greenhouse, perhaps by the door. Another week, and they can be removed to a cold frame. More air may gradually be admitted to the frame until the seedlings only receive protection at night. Planting can only take place when all possible danger of frost in the garden is past.

As you see, many half-hardy annuals need heat to germinate, followed by several weeks of warm, light, protected conditions. Then, during the slow process of hardening off, the young plants are still going to need warm nights. So, unless you have a heated greenhouse or conservatory, it is advisable to buy these plants (see page 99).

Herbaceous perennials

Many herbaceous perennials can be increased from seed. Most cultivars will not come true, but you may well end up with an interesting result. The method is the same as for half-hardy annuals, but instead of pricking them out into trays, they should be potted individually in 3 in. pots, and may even need potting again before they are large enough to be planted in the border. They should be hardened off in the same manner as described above. For hardy annuals, see page 73.

Sowing seeds

Unless you need a large quantity of plants, it is unnecessary to sow a whole seed tray—you can use a half-tray or a clean 3 in. pot. Fill with fresh seed compost and firm the compost gently so that it is within ½ in. or less from the top. Scatter seed very thinly over the surface and sieve a little more compost on top using a fine-mesh sieve. According to the temperature recommended on the seed packet, put the tray or pots either in the airing cupboard, on the kitchen windowsill or in a propagator or greenhouse.

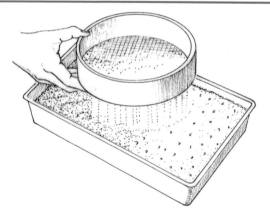

Scatter seed thinly over the compost, then sieve a little more compost on top.

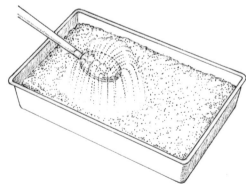

Water, using a fine rose, until the surface of the compost is thoroughly damp.

Obtaining rarer plants from seed

There is nothing more tantalizing than seeing a photograph of some desirable plant and not being able to get hold of it. There are numerous reasons why a plant is rare—it may be hard to propagate or it may lack pot appeal (in other words it looks unattractive in its pot at the garden center). If it does not sell, nurserymen lose interest, the plant becomes scarcer and the cycle continues. Or perhaps you live in some out-of-the-way place where only a limited range of plants is available or you may find it hard to import plants. But there are rarely any restrictions on importing packets of seed through the mail, and by growing plants from seed you will suddenly have access to a vast new range of trees, shrubs, herbaceous plants and alpines. You may need to join specialist societies and send off for their catalogs to see what is available as seed.

As regards the best time to sow, this is probably immediately after the seed arrives. If the seed does not germinate in the first spring after sowing, it may well do so in the second. Try and find out what sort of climate the plant comes from in the wild. If you have seed of a plant you know little about, try sowing half the seed in warmth and the other half outside. Seeds from plants native to the temperate regions often need a period of freezing weather (as they would have had in the wild) in order to germinate. Some, such as peonies, can take a year or more to come up, and it is not until you are just about to throw the pot away that you notice the seedlings. By this time a soil-less compost would have become compacted, so make a mixture of two parts soil-based seed compost and one part sharp sand or sharp grit to assist drainage; since the pot will be outside in all weathers, it is important that it does not become waterlogged.

Use a clean 3 in. pot. Fill it to within ½ in. of the rim with the compost and firm gently with the base of another pot. Sow the seeds as thinly as possible—there is less danger of damaging the seedlings when transplanting if they are uncrowded. Sieve a very thin layer of soil over the top, about the depth of the seed itself, then put about ½ in. of grit on top of the pot (unless the seed is very fine). This prevents liverworts and moss from establishing themselves and conserves moisture. Water through a fine rose. Label the pot with the name of the plant and the date of sowing.

Place the pot in a shady place and water it now and again in hot weather. Success is not guaranteed, but you cannot imagine the joy of seeing a peony seedling appear, after waiting patiently for two years. If the seed germinates in early spring, and the weather is cold and wet, move the pot to a cool greenhouse or frame for protection. As soon as the seeds have their first true leaves, they may be potted individually.

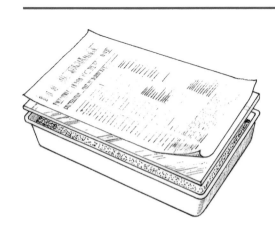

Lay over a pane of glass covered by a sheet of newspaper and keep warm.

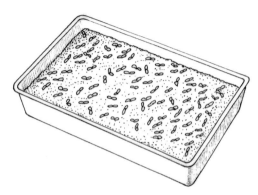

Remove glass and paper as soon as seedlings appear. Allow them plenty of light.

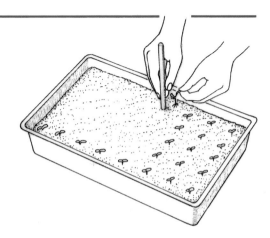

When the seedlings have a pair of leaves, prick them out into trays 2 in. apart.

Supporting your plants

Peonies (Paeonia lactiflora cultivars) are most easily supported with metal hoops as seen on the left of the picture. The delphiniums and lilies in the background would also need staking to stop them falling forward. In a well-staked border you should barely see the supports.

However colorful a vista your flower border presents, if it is littered with assorted stakes, many of them protruding above the plants, the whole effect will be spoilt. Supporting your plants is something to be approached with care and a little ingenuity. However, in a closely planted flower bed, many plants will gain support by leaning on their neighbors, and it is remarkable how many tall herbaceous plants require no staking; such plants include *Macleaya*, *Arundo donax*, *Aconitum × carmichaelii* 'Arendsii,' tall phloxes and *Eupatorium maculatum*.

You should choose your time to stake carefully, and with regard to the plant in question. Delphiniums, for example, when the shoots are about 1½ ft. high, could have the clump supported with a metal hoop or with brand-name wire supports, which are comparatively unobtrusive. A few weeks later, when the flower stems are rapidly gaining height and the plants are burgeoning with lush growth, you could start using taller stakes.

For the sort of delphiniums you see at flower shows, each flower spike should have an individual stake, but usually these and other large herbaceous perennials can be staked as follows: put in a number of canes around the clump (trying not to pierce the roots), attach green garden string to them and weave it in and out and back and forth between the flower stems. Supported this way, the plants appear more natural. Brittle, succulent stems, secured too tightly to a cane, will snap at the point of attachment when the wind blows, so it is better to tie them loosely, making a figure eight with the stake and flower stem, leaving room for a little movement. Dahlias, with their mass of leafage, usually need something stronger than bamboo canes: wooden stakes about 1 in. square are appropriate.

Many plants can be allowed to flop gently about, but should they start leaning too far, an excellent method of support consists of a semi-circle of metal, with long legs that push into the ground, a boon to anybody with an aversion to staking. Painted matt black or dark green, you hardly notice them, and they are quick and easy to put in place. Supports with legs about 3 ft. long are good for tall perennials, while those about 1 ft. are excellent for the discreet control of bulging plants on the edge of a bed. Even shrub roses sometimes need support, and two of these metal hoops placed around the plant to form a circle can be left in place from year to year. Twiggy branches (such as those of hazel, often used for culinary peas) can be pushed into the soil to support leafy clumps of herbaceous plants. One of the least obtrusive forms of staking (they are quickly concealed as the plants grow), they are excellent, and cheap—if you can get them.

As with all garden tasks, work ethic comes in particularly handy with regard to staking. Inventing excuses, like having to go back and fetch the string or the stakes, is a pretext to put off this essential job.

Buying plants

To give your plants the best chance to establish in your own garden, be very particular when buying. Try and reject pot-bound or very recently potted specimens, and insist on healthy foliage without signs of pest or disease. Peonies (Paeonia lactiflora cultivars), curry plant (Helichrysum italicum) and Viola cornuta are seen here.

deserve a good start to their short summer lives, so the discerning shopper will insist on bushy plants, with healthy green leaves, and will wait until the weather has warmed up before buying them.

With all container-grown plants, you have to ask yourself how long the plant has been in its pot. Lift up the pot to see whether the plant has rooted through the drainage hole. A few roots poking through show the plant is well established in its pot. A large mat of roots indicates that the plant has been there too long and its roots have become pot-bound; in this case there will be signs of starvation, with stunted growth and yellowish leaves. There may be weeds such as annuals, grasses and hairy bittercress growing on the surface. If a tree or shrub has got to this stage, it may never grow properly.

Quite the reverse is the case of a small plant in a large pot, which may well have only been there for a week or so. The whole idea of containers is that plants are so well established (without being pot-bound) they hardly notice the move to your garden. But as soon as you take such a plant out of its container, the potting medium will fall away, leaving you with a small plant that will be slow to settle.

With trees and shrubs, shape is important. Make sure the plant is well balanced, with plenty of healthy shoots and no snags or dead wood or signs of chafing on the stem. Evergreens should have glossy, healthy foliage, with no shriveled edges to the leaves, which may indicate that the plant has been sitting about in an icy spring wind. There should be no sign of the ticket-collector: a neat little U-shaped notch in the leaf, about ¼ in. wide, a typical bite of the adult vine weevil.

Some herbaceous plants, pinks (*Dianthus*) and violas for example, are better bought as young non-flowering plants, in small pots. If the plant is sprawling over the sides of a large pot, and has clearly been flowering for some time, especially if it has started to form seed heads, it is over the top.

When buying *Clematis* or other soft-stemmed climbers, make sure that the supporting cane has not been dislodged, damaging the stems at the base.

Buying plants is an art in itself. The plants you see for sale have all been raised in the optimum conditions for fast, healthy growth. But a lot depends on what has happened to them between the time of leaving the nursery where they were raised and the time you buy them. Have a good look at the plants in the garden center with a critical eye to ensure that you are buying a healthy specimen.

To extend the season of the bedding-plant business you will often see petunias, begonias and *Impatiens* shivering outside a shop far too early in spring—they will take some time to recover from such a check to growth. Likewise, at the end of the season there will be plants that have been far too long in their trays, easily recognized by their spindly stems and yellowing leaves. Half-hardy annuals

THROUGH
THE SEASONS

I have always felt that the flower gardener's year divides naturally into eight, rather than four, seasons, and this is how the gardening year is presented here. While beginners to gardening may be given confidence by precise dates, deciding when to sow or plant depends much more on closely observing your garden and the general look of the plants, as well as taking into account your local weather conditions. From one year to the next, the start of a season can vary by several weeks, and a few miles can make all the difference to air and soil temperatures. Seasonal highlights that are mentioned throughout this chapter may well inspire you to try out some new and special plant.

Campanula latiloba *'Hidcote Amethyst' and foxgloves* (Digitalis), *seen beneath a canopy of old roses, conjure up an image of high summer. Many flower gardens are at their best in summer, but every season has its own appeal—as well as its essential tasks.*

Early spring

Snowdrops and crocuses, opening their flowers to the sun, will tempt you outdoors. Early daffodils—*Narcissus* 'Tête-à-Tête,' 'February Silver' and 'February Gold'—are in full flower and bare earth is being transformed into a carpet of small bulbs: ice-blue *Puschkinia scilloides*, glistening yellow *Eranthis hyemalis* (winter aconite) and *Scilla bifolia* in different shades of blue as well as pink. Plants of wallflowers and winter pansies, already dotted with flowers, will be filling out in the warm air. *Viburnum farreri* is already a haze of green, and little rosettes of shining young leaves decorate the branches of *Hydrangea anomala petiolaris*.

The hellebore season is reaching its zenith. *Helleborus orientalis* hybrids—all beautiful, but some especially so—can be found with flowers plain or spotted, faintly speckled or heavily mottled. Their colors can be luminous white, primrose and pale pink through to maroon and purple, perhaps the most alluring being the darkest shades, like the almost blue-black 'Philip Ballard.' Lovers of rich soil and cool positions, they may be divided now or just after flowering. *H. argutifolius* (Corsican hellebore), *H. foetidus* and *H. viridis* add to the assortment with flowers of light green to emerald.

A patch of *Primula vulgaris sibthorpii* (just like our wild primrose but a pretty mauve-pink) will light up a group of dark purple hellebores. Lungworts or *Pulmonaria*, old-fashioned herbaceous plants long established in our gardens, also look well intermingled with hellebores. Apart from *Pulmonaria officinalis*, with spotted leaves and flowers in a medley of pink and blue, there are many good cultivars such as *P.* 'Roy Davidson,' with azure flowers, or brick-red *P. rubra* 'David Ward,' with leaves smartly variegated in cream and green.

Foolhardy tree peonies are fattening their buds, quite unaware of how capricious the

Snowdrops, crocuses and emerging hellebores herald the beginning of spring.

weather can be at this time. It is easy for us to be misled, like the peony, and start sowing or planting too early, but, keeping an eye on the weather and soil temperature, you can start sowing hardy annuals now (see page 73) and prepare the flower beds (see page 81). Under glass, pot up tender perennials that were rooted last autumn (see page 93) and sow half-hardy annuals (see page 96). Plant out autumn-sown sweet peas (*Lathyrus odoratus*).

However tidy you left the garden in autumn, winter debris—desiccated leaves, twigs that seem to have come from nowhere, stems of herbaceous plants forgotten then—will have accumulated over the winter. Lightly fork over the flower beds, tidying and weeding as you go. Spread over general fertilizer and bonemeal and rake them in. Remove any protective winter covering from tender plants. Plant all hardy plants—trees, shrubs, perennials and roses —provided the weather is clement and the soil is not sodden.

Prune roses (see page 88), feed with a general fertilizer (or a rose fertilizer) and bonemeal.

Aphids love to hide among the leaves of pinks (*Dianthus*); spray with insecticide if you find them. When you lift up the mats of *Dianthus* foliage, you may well also find colonies of over-wintering slugs. Pick them off and dispose of them. Other slugs will be regrouping near hostas about to come into leaf, so scatter slugbait around their crowns.

Snowdrops (*Galanthus*) should be divided as soon as they have finished flowering. Started off from dry bulbs in autumn, they take some time to settle down and they should be moved when in growth, known as "in the green." As they love woodland conditions they can be planted under deciduous trees and shrubs, or around herbaceous perennials that are rarely moved, such as *Smilacina* and *Kirengeshoma*, or at the back of a border. Every three years or so dig up and divide your clumps, working in some leaf mold and bonemeal, and replant two or three bulbs together in little groups to make more of a show for the following year.

Plant summer bulbs—*Galtonia*, *Allium* and *Gladioli*—in a sunny place and lilies in sun or part-shade. Organize a potful of *Gladiolus callianthus* to place near where you sit in the sun; their elegant white flowers with maroon centers and heady, sweet scent will revive you in late summer. Except in very mild climates they should be lifted in autumn, dried off and stored under frost-free conditions.

On poor soils *Galtonia candicans* (summer hyacinth), from South Africa, may have to be renewed quite often by fresh bulbs, but their 3 ft. spires of fragrant white dangling bells provide cool relief in late summer. Two temptresses in lime-green, both easy from seed, are *Galtonia princeps* and *G. viridiflora*. Useful for interplanting with early-flowering herbaceous plants, they all need rich, well-drained soil in sun.

Lilies are perhaps the most beautiful of summer bulbs. But one must be very fussy when shopping for them: the bulbs should feel fresh and plump and their roots full of life. Lilies like a loose, crumbly consistency to the soil, so before planting them work in compost, well-rotted manure or leaf mold and plenty of bonemeal. Some lilies, for example *Lilium regale*, are easy from seed and this is the way to get a good stock of healthy bulbs. Established lilies should be mulched now, with a light covering of leaf mold or well-rotted compost to protect the young shoots from frost.

Neither *Lilium auratum* (golden-rayed lily of Japan) nor *Lilium speciosum* like lime in the soil, but they do well in pots. Although they may deteriorate after a year or two, they provide such beautiful adornment to our terraces that they are worth replacing often. For potting, a mixture of roughly three parts good soil, one of leaf mold and half a part of grit should make a nice open compost. Be sparing with water to begin with, as they do not enjoy soggy conditions.

Dahlia tubers that have been in store can be propagated now, provided you have a greenhouse or conservatory. The old tubers can be encouraged to send out young shoots by spraying with water. When the shoots are about 3 – 4 in. long cut them off cleanly with a knife and root them in cuttings compost (see page 92). Cover them with a polyethylene tent or glass jar to encourage them to root quickly.

Hard-prune *Perovskia*, *Ceratostigma willmottianum* and hardy fuchsias to within a few inches of ground level and *Caryopteris* × *clandonensis*, *Buddleia davidii* and *Hydrangea paniculata* 'Grandiflora' to within one or two buds of the previous season's growth. Trim and tidy *Santolina*, *Artemisia*, *Lavatera* and *Penstemon* and prune *Romneya coulteri* (Californian tree poppy) to within 1 ft. from the ground. In cold areas, wait a few more weeks before doing this.

Tulips and scillas mean warmer soil and longer days, when spring is well underway.

Spring

As spring arrives on a warm breeze with occasional gentle rain, the sun rises higher in the sky, breathing new life into the soil, warming and drying its surface. Aware of the change of season, suddenly everything seems to be growing apace, including the weeds.

Hurry to finish planting all hardy plants, taking advantage of the good growing weather. If the soil is dry, fill the planting hole with water, put in the young plant, and cover it with soil immediately—moisture close to the plant's roots will help it to establish quickly; water overhead as well. Divide Michaelmas daisies (*Aster novi-belgii* cultivars), *Monarda*, *Kniphofia*, *Schizostylis* and ornamental grasses. In mild areas plant dahlia tubers, incorporating well-rotted compost and bonemeal in the bottom of the planting hole.

If you are putting on a mulch, make sure the ground is clean of weeds beforehand. This is an ideal time for mulching, as the soil should still be moist (if it is not, water thoroughly) after winter, but has started to warm up. Mulch roses, clematis, herbaceous plants and newly planted trees and shrubs with compost and well-rotted manure, to conserve moisture and prevent weeds from germinating.

Continue to sow hardy annuals outside, and plant out young sweet peas (*Lathyrus odoratus*). Sow further batches of half-hardy annuals in warmth, and start hardening off those sown earlier. If cold nights are expected, cover the cold frame with an old blanket or burlap to keep out frost. In the greenhouse or conservatory take extra care over ventilation on hot days, shade young seedlings and damp down the floor by swilling cans of water over it—this reduces the temperature temporarily and adds moisture to the air, thus creating a nice growing atmosphere for seedlings.

Spray roses with an appropriate combined insecticide and fungicide against aphids, blackspot and mildew; always follow the manufacturers' instructions. This needs to be done at regular intervals during summer. In town gardens especially, you may need to include lilies and wall plants in your spraying program. To blast the aphids into eternity, aim the nozzle of the spray at the undersurface of the leaves as well as the top. You may not want to use chemical sprays, in which case the best protection you can offer your plants is good cultivation: a well-grown, well-nourished plant has natural resistance to pests and diseases.

Start preparing containers for summer bedding plants, so that they will be ready for planting as soon as all danger of frost is past. Soil-less composts are fine for the duration of the summer, but if you intend to plant permanent specimens such as *Camellia* or *Hydrangea*, soil-based compost has more substance and is less likely to compact. A layer of drainage is essential: put broken pieces of clay pot, mixed rubble or gravel in the base first.

Whereas the leaves of snowdrops and crocuses fade quietly away in late spring, those of the larger daffodils can be very obtrusive. Either grow the prettier, smaller *Narcissus* like 'Hawera,' 'Tête-à-Tête,' 'February Gold,' 'Peeping Tom,' 'Dove Wings,' and the rare pale yellow old cultivar 'Eystettensis,' or grow the larger cultivars near the back of the flower bed, so that taller plants will grow up and hide them. Try interplanting them with *Astilbe*, whose feathery foliage will camouflage the dying leaves, or among Japanese anemones (*Anemone × hybrida*). If you find you have put them in the wrong place, or they have become overcrowded and need dividing, daffodils move well after flowering. Make a hole with the trowel, mix in some bonemeal, drop the bulb in, fill up with water and replace the soil. Mark their position carefully with small canes, to ensure that they are not dug up by mistake when dormant.

An extravagant attitude helps when it comes to tulips. Their rather formal flowers look just right lavishly grouped in your borders, forming vivid patches of color among the different spring greens of perennial plants, whereas other bulbs seem more in keeping with the wilder, more natural parts of the garden. On some soils tulips do not last many years (it is said that planting them deeply helps them to last longer), so build up your collection by buying more each autumn. The early cultivars such as *Tulipa* 'Heart's Delight,' 'Shakespeare' and 'Red Riding Hood' flower before the main spring display and later ones are invaluable for extending color into early summer.

In spring, amid all the bustle and rush to keep up with the garden, time must be found to stop and wonder at it all. Otherwise you might miss some of the more ephemeral flowers of the season such as primroses and their relatives —cowslips, polyanthus and auriculas.

As spring turns into summer Rosa *'Bonica'* and Lychnis coronaria *are in full flower.*

Late spring and early summer

Gardening at this season is a never-ending rush of activity: by the time you have done the weeding, mowed the lawn, edged the grass, swept the paths, sprayed the aphids, baited the slugs, dead-headed the daffodils, pricked out the seedlings, and watered all the young plants—you usually need to start all over again.

If the weather is warm and settled, half-hardy annuals, tender perennials and young dahlias can be planted out now, provided you are quite certain there will be no frost. Continue sowing hardy annuals outside and half-hardy annuals in warmth, and harden off those sown earlier. If you want to make way for summer bedding, carefully lift tulips with a fork and replant them in an out-of-the-way spot to die down naturally. From now till autumn spray roses every few weeks with a combined

insecticide and fungicide. Dead-head tulips and daffodils, but leave smaller bulbs, such as grape hyacinths (*Muscari*), *Scilla*, *Chionodoxa*, dog's-tooth violets (*Erythronium*) and snowdrops (*Galanthus*), to seed themselves.

Herbaceous lobelias, such as *Lobelia cardinalis*, can be divided now into small rosettes of leaves and replanted with compost and general fertilizer. Start staking tall perennials such as delphiniums. Consider how you could improve your early-summer garden for next year, by having a look at the list of plants that flower now (see page 54).

Make more plans for next year by sowing some biennials in a nursery bed outside, or in pots under glass: wallflowers (*Cheiranthus cheiri*), sweet Williams (*Dianthus barbatus*), foxgloves (*Digitalis purpurea*), stocks (*Matthiola*), forget-me-nots (*Myosotis*), Iceland poppies (*Papaver nudicaule*) and Canterbury bells (*Campanula medium*). *Eryngium giganteum* does not transplant well and is better sown *in situ*.

Plant containers as soon as there is no danger of frost. Many summer bedding plants have rather boring leaves, so to invent a pretty composition in a pot, remember to plant some good foliage as a suitable foil to the flowers. For an exuberant, tropical effect use *Melianthus major*, a tender shrubby plant with superb, very large, blue-gray pinnate leaves and purple cannas (*Canna indica* 'Purpurea'). Three of the best in silver are lacy-leaved *Senecio vira-vira*, *Helichrysum petiolare* that weaves its silvery stems in and out of nearby plants, and *Plecostachys serpyllifolia*, which does the same as the *Helichrysum* but on a much smaller scale. *Fuchsia magellanica* 'Versicolor,' small-leaved variegated ivies and hostas, particularly the large-leaved glaucous *Hosta sieboldiana* 'Elegans,' would all be excellent in shade.

Plant *Crinum* now—handsome, bulbous plants that need deep, rich, well-drained soil by a sunny wall.

Summer

Whatever sort of garden you have, at mid-summer it will seem to fall under a spell. Plants assume the glossy look of exuberant health with the long days and warm nights. Oriental poppies unfold their buds of crinkled silk, peonies burst into voluptuous blossom, and an air of expectancy hovers over the garden as roses prepare to join the summer fête. Lupins and delphiniums, campanulas and irises, honeysuckles and sweet peas, larkspurs and Madonna lilies, plants from the queen of lady's slipper orchids, *Cypripedium reginae*, to the common *Alchemilla mollis*—such beauty demands time for contemplation.

But after this brief pause, three words should ring constantly in your head—"weeding, watering, dead-heading." As the days begin to shorten imperceptibly, how good your garden looks greatly depends on these three operations. But they do give you an excuse to do an immense amount of dawdling up and down, admiring the flowers, and studying the singular personality of each plant. A pinch here and a snip there, down to the compost heap and back again—it seems that at this season gardening is mainly wandering around with hand shears and a bucket. But by observing your plants closely, you will notice one that clashes with its neighbor (make a note to move it), one that is looking rather weak (might it like a liquid feed?), or yet another in urgent need of insecticide.

Summer is a time to dream, and it is hard to think of next spring now. But for primroses to flourish they must be divided, and moved to a different position. Another advantage of transplanting them is that you stay one jump ahead of the vine weevil whose grubs are specially fond of members of the genus *Primula*. When dividing primrose roots (see page 91), work crumbled old manure, compost or leaf mold into the hole, and dust with bonemeal.

*Rudbeckias, Chinese lantern (*Physalis*) and goldenrod (*Solidago*) mark the shorter days.*

Bearded irises need dividing every three years or so. About six weeks after flowering, if you dig one up and have a look, you will see that it is starting to form fat new roots. This is the moment for division. Lift the plants with a fork and discard the old central rhizomes. Replant the younger, outer rhizomes in enriched soil, placing them on the surface and firming the soil around the roots. Then cut the top of the leaves off by at least half (or the wind could dislodge the plant). Irises insist on a sunny position and decent soil.

To persuade delphiniums to bloom again in autumn, cut the plants to the ground as soon as the flowers fade. Work in a generous handful of fertilizer per plant, water lavishly, mulch with manure and protect from slugs. After the first flush of bloom, feed roses with a general or rose fertilizer and keep up the spraying program.

Staking (see page 98) is so much better done before the plant falls down, rather than after —try to anticipate which plants need support.

Late summer and early autumn

Late summer brings sultry days and hot, drying winds. Plants are burgeoning with growth, laden with a mass of thirsting leaves. Foliage has a sere and dusty look and to keep the garden sparkling in late summer extra time should be reserved for tidying up all the little bits and pieces of vegetable clutter such as leaves and fallen petals clustering in corners. Snip the odd yellowing leaf and cut back the stems of early-flowering herbaceous perennials.

Although there may be a lull in weed growth (until autumn rains charm the umpteenth batch of weed seeds into germination), the treadmill of watering and dead-heading spins even faster. And think of all the plants that are still to reach their peak, some of which well appreciate a little fussing over with liquid feed—chrysanthemums, (*Dendranthema*), Japanese anemones (*Anemone × hybrida*), *Kirengeshoma*, *Eupatorium*, toad lilies (*Tricyrtis*), *Aster*, *Crocosmia*, *Amaryllis belladonna* and many other plants that truly belong to autumn. Containers, now thickly filled with foraging roots, will need even more attention with watering and liquid feed, to sustain the plants during their final fling.

Take cuttings of tender perennials and shrubs (see page 92) and of pinks (see page 94). If you can harden your heart and chop *Viola* hard back (which means taking off all the flowers), you will encourage them to make masses of ideal shoots for cuttings (see page 94). Experiment with taking cuttings of many different plants, including alpines and shrubs.

Prune away the flowered stems of rambling roses and tie in the young shoots—if there are not enough, leave on some of the old ones.

It is time to start thinking about bulbs and where to plant them. Daffodils start to grow early in autumn and should be planted now.

Autumn

Early autumn with its warm, still days is the most magic of seasons: cooler nights refresh the plants, the harsh brilliance has gone out of the sun and a gentler, slower mood enters the garden. After such *embarras de richesse* of summer, there is something rather touching about autumn flowers; they seem all the more desirable as they; brighten the waning year. Colors glow in the softer light, heavy dew revives heat-worn plants, leaving little diamonds on the lawn in the morning and bespangling the fluffy mauve flower-heads of *Pennisetum orientale* (quite the prettiest grass) with drops of moisture.

New ideas to consider, new plans to pore over, new plants to be listed, new beds to be made, a chance to make good all the mistakes —this, the beginning of the gardening year, is a most exhilarating and creative time.

The great autumn tidy

Gardening, as any other aspect of life, is all a matter of choice and you should choose plants that you can grow well, so that they may flourish and you may enjoy looking at them where they are placed. So go around the garden slowly now, with a clear head, paper and pencil, and carefully consider each plant.

Ask yourself if you really like it? It may be a plant you inherited in the garden, and you have got so used to its presence that you never even see it, let alone wonder whether or not to get rid of it. Or maybe it was a plant you bought in a fit of enthusiasm, when you thought gaudy variegation or two-tone flowers were the very thing. Perhaps the plant had an enticing catalog description, but in reality is rather drab.

Still standing beside the same plant, ask yourself the second question: does it need propagating? Perhaps it is such a nice plant that you would like more of it; if so, take a cutting, collect seed, or divide it up and make a lovely

Autumn-flowering Cyclamen hederifolium *with their mottled leaves.*

large group of it. Conversely, having become more discriminating about plants, you may have decided you do not like it. In which case, the plant still needs propagating, in order that you can salve your conscience by giving away a rooted cutting or small division.

The third, possibly the most important question to ask yourself is: is the plant in the right place? Is it happy in the soil and position where it is growing? Perhaps it would prefer a damper, or a drier, spot? Has it got enough room to display itself properly? It may be that it is being elbowed out by a strong-growing neighbor, or alternatively it is smothering some delicate treasure. And does it enhance, or detract from, plants growing nearby, with regard to its height, shape and color?

Many plants have a limited lifespan—lavenders (*Lavandula*), *Daphne*, *Cistus*, for example. So the next question to consider is the general health of the plant. Is it flowering as well as last year? Perhaps it is beginning to

deteriorate, becoming old and woody, in which case you would be much better off to take a cutting and replace the aged specimen with a new young plant.

Autumn is a splendid time to make all these adjustments: you can still see exactly what size and color a plant is, whereas in spring many plants are just tuffets of foliage at ground level. It is excellent transplanting weather, as the soil is still warm; and furthermore it is one of the best times for taking cuttings.

Plant bulbs, shrubs, herbaceous plants, roses and biennials. Continue spraying roses and check the ties on climbing roses. Divide lilies and plant new ones as soon as available. Plant out rooted pink cuttings. Continue cutting back herbaceous plants. Take out summer bedding as it goes over and plant spring bedding plants. When planting spring bedding, do not overfeed with manure at this time of year, as it would only encourage soft growth, likely to be damaged by frost—a sprinkling of bonemeal is all that is required. Take cuttings of tender perennials and move pots of tender plants under glass.

Take out all summer plants from containers, even if they are still flowering. This will give the spring show of wallflowers, forget-me-nots, primroses, winter pansies and stocks (in mild areas) a chance to get well settled in before winter. If the containers were filled with fresh compost at the beginning of the season, there is no need to change the soil, just loosen it up and give a sprinkling of bonemeal.

When planting a container with bulbs, plant for a succession of flowers: put crocuses, daffodils (both early and late) and tulips (both early and late) all in the same container. Plant the bulbs at different levels according to their size—in other words the largest daffodils at the deepest level and little bulbs, such as crocuses, nearer the surface. For suggestions about bulbs to naturalize in grass, see page 75.

Late autumn

Late autumn is a mess of bedraggled herbaceous plants, muddy paths, and flurries of leaves swirling around and forming soggy little heaps. In large gardens, consisting mainly of trees and shrubs, ground-cover plants and bulbs, the leaves can remain where they fall and be gradually drawn down by worms to feed the soil. But in small gardens, many herbaceous plants and alpines do not appreciate wet, leafy dishcloths tucked around their necks, and it is much better to collect them—at the same time you greatly reduce the slug population by picking up those hiding in the leaf litter. If all the dividing and transplanting has been done a month or so ago, you can now give your whole attention to tidying. Finally, lightly fork over the flower beds.

Lift dahlias. Cut them back and stand the tubers in a shed so that the succulent ends of the stems can dry out, then store them in boxes in a frost-free place with a light covering of peat. Check them now and again and cut away any pieces of rotten tuber. If you find they have dried out too much, soak them in water to plump them up. Lift gladioli and hang them to dry in a warm, well-ventilated place. Sow sweet peas outside, or in pots in a cold frame.

When the weather is suitable, plant shrubs, herbaceous plants, roses, biennials and bulbs. The earlier in autumn bulbs are planted the better, but tulips can be planted up to mid-winter. Dig and manure new beds (see page 81). Cut back topgrowth of roses (see page 88).

Protect tender plants on walls with an eiderdown made of bubblewrap supported by wire netting and secured to it with plant ties, or with polyethylene sheeting supported by canes. Insert some twiggy branches or bamboo canes between the plant and its protective covering, so that air can circulate. Alpines that resent winter wet should be covered with glass.

Crocus tommasinianus *peep through the snow before winter is over.*

Mid-winter

It is in winter, when the fancy dress of summer has fallen away, that you will understand the need for good structure—good evergreens, balanced shape and height of trees and shrubs, strong lines of paths and pleasing shapes of lawns and flower beds. It is now that one most appreciates the green background provided by holly, yew, *Viburnum tinus* and box. The demure flowers of winter, such as the cream bells, delicately speckled with red inside, of *Clematis cirrhosa balearica*, are perfectly attuned to the low light.

Winter-flowering heathers (*Erica carnea*) form drifts of pink and white, bulbs are beginning to push through the earth and *Iris unguicularis* will be putting on an extravagant display of fragile lavender blooms under your warmest wall. In sheltered gardens *Daphne bholua* will be starting to produce its rosy-mauve clusters of flower and spreading scent all around. But the winter apparel of the flower garden is mostly a pattern of leaves—polished silver, gray felt, acid-green spikes, blue-green and copper-bronze—all these colors and textures diluted by the watery sun to the muted winter palette.

As soon as the weather turns really cold, the leaves of *Bergenia purpurascens* change from green to dark beetroot-red, with a lighter red reverse. The oatlike flower-heads on bleached stems of the grass *Stipa gigantea*, a masterpiece of airy grace, are still beautiful in their skeletal stage. Cascades of wandlike stems are dotted in the starry-yellow flowers of the winter jasmine (*Jasminum nudiflorum*). Try planting this essential winter shrub close to one of the hybrid musk roses, such as *Rosa* 'Buff Beauty,' to get two seasons of flower from the same patch.

It is worth searching for a good, large-flowered form of the true Christmas rose, *Helleborus niger*. It is a variable species and you want one that lives up to its name as regards flowering time. Cover the plant with a cloche to protect its sumptuous white flowers from mud.

Arum italicum italicum, its dark green leaves with a satiny sheen, prominently marbled in gray-green, gives a cheerful account of itself in winter. It is wonderful for picking when there is little fresh foliage around, is happy in poor soil and it has fat little stalks topped with pale scarlet berries in autumn.

Hurry to finish all digging (see page 81) if the weather is reasonable, so the soil is exposed to frost which will break it down to a crumbly tillage. If possible, order some manure, cover it with a sheet of polyethylene and leave it to mature so that it is ready for spring planting. Finish planting trees, shrubs and roses.

Tidy the garden shed, clean and sharpen your tools. In greenhouses and conservatories water sparingly, look over the plants regularly and remove decaying leaves. Order your seed catalogs, and sit down in front of the fire planning next year.

KEY PLANTS FOR THE FLOWER GARDEN

To choose but fifty plants from the fifty thousand plants in cultivation today is not easy, but then the essence of good gardening is selection. So before buying any one of these plants, ask yourself where you are going to place it. Is it going to be happy in your soil and growing conditions? Will it complement your color scheme? Using this list as a starting point—there are countless other equally worthy plants you could grow—you will find that each plant is either a component of the flower garden when in bloom, or that it contributes something special by way of its long-flowering season or its good foliage. Or it may simply be desirable for the minor role it plays in the garden pageant.

Hardy geraniums—seen here are Geranium psilostemon *and* G. endressii—*are some of the most reliable and longest-flowering plants for the flower garden. Roses have their moment of glory too, though it is often shorter-lived, but Rosa 'Wilhelm,' seen here, flowers almost continuously throughout the summer.*

The plants in the following list are mostly herbaceous perennials, the backbone of the flower garden. When you add a sound framework of shrubs, some essential roses, annuals for changing patches of excitement here and there and, of course, bulbs, you can gradually compose your garden picture. The majority are favorite old garden flowers, renowned for reliable behavior, but there are a few tempting plants that are relatively scarce. A plant may be rare for several reasons—it could be that it is rather difficult and requires very precise growing conditions, or perhaps it has remained unsung because it is endowed with a complicated name, which itself keeps changing. There are several plants on the list that are not to be found in every garden center, but they warrant the little extra searching required.

Under each plant listed there is a note about the propagation it requires. If this does not mention division, and only refers to "cuttings" or "seed," you can assume the parent plant should be left undisturbed.

Baptisia australis

Alchemilla mollis
(Lady's mantle)

Whether spilling over the front of borders, running around beneath the skirts of old roses, or tucked into odd shady corners the fluffy mounds of tiny lime-green flowers, produced in early summer, seem to blend with any color scheme. Indispensable and obliging, it will often cloak your mistakes by uniting a formerly random mix of plants, and is marvelous for filling up gaps when starting a garden. It can be relegated to spaces between paving stones, shady gravel or as ground cover beneath shrubs as you find other plants for the choice spots. A wild self-seeder, as soon as the flowers fade it should be ruthlessly cut back, leaves and all: the plant will quickly renew itself into a low mound of pretty, soft green silky foliage. Good for picking. Native to western Asia.

Size H: 6 in.; S: 1 ft. **Aspect** From full sun to deep shade. **Soil** Any, unless waterlogged. **Propagation** Division or seed. **Planting partners** Anything, but especially good with purple foliage. Interplant with early bulbs.

Allium christophii

A highly decorative onion member of the lily family, not least because of its shape *Allium christophii* has immense globular heads of starry little amethyst flowers on 2 ft. stems in mid-summer, followed by sensational seed heads. The plant's silhouette, like a large ball of stars perched on a stick, makes a wonderful contrast in form with plants that form silvery mats, such as *Artemisia stelleriana*, and low-growing herbaceous plants, to help disguise the foliage which dies off as the flowers emerge. It will self-seed, and until your colony is large enough you should resist the temptation to pick the seed heads until after they have dropped their shiny black seeds. Good for picking and seed heads for drying. Native to Iran, Turkey and Central Asia.

Size H: 2 ft.; S: 1½ ft. **Aspect** Full sun. **Soil** Rich in organic matter, well drained. **Propagation** Division or seed. **Planting partners** Silver-leaved plants.

Anaphalis triplinervis
(Pearl everlasting)

Rare among silver-leaved plants, this will grow in light shade, even in damp ground, because it comes from the Himalayas, where it grows in wet meadows and on the edge of open woodland. It has little pearly-white everlasting flowers over neat rosettes of gray foliage which remains decorative for most of the year. Flowers in late summer and autumn and is very useful when you want to introduce silver foliage to a border in part-shade. Good for picking and drying. Native of Afghanistan to southwest China.

Size H: 15 in.; S: 2 ft. **Aspect** Sun or part-shade. **Soil** Most, if not too dry. **Propagation** Division every few years. **Planting partners** *Sedum* 'Vera Jameson' and 'Herbstfreude,' *Aster × frikartii* 'Mönch.'

Anemone × hybrida
'Honorine Jobert'
(Japanese anemone)

Tolerating widely diverse types of soil and position, bothered neither by pest nor disease, needing no staking or regular division, this lovely plant is not grown just for ease of maintenance, but for its beautiful, rounded cup-shaped pure white flowers with yellow middles, one of the delights of early autumn. An invaluable plant, initially slow, it may become invasive once established.

Size H: 5 ft.; S: 2 ft. **Aspect** Sun or shade. **Soil** Any, provided drainage is good. **Propagation** Division, but may be left in position for years. **Planting partners** *Eupatorium maculatum atropurpureum*, *Hydrangea*, *Fuchsia*. Also interplant with early bulbs.

Angel's fishing rod see *Dierama pulcherrimum*

Anthemis tinctoria
'E.C. Buxton'

A pretty pale yellow daisy (unlike most yellow daisies, which come in brassier tones) with much-cut ferny leaves, useful for soft color schemes in summer. Apt to flower itself to death if not dead-headed regularly and renewed often by cuttings. Good for picking.

Size H and S: 3 ft. **Aspect** Sun. **Soil** Well drained. **Propagation** Cuttings. **Planting partners** Blue flowers, wonderful with *Salvia × superba*.

Aster × frikartii
'Mönch'
(Michaelmas daisy)

For a seemingly endless supply of lavender-blue daisies with yellow centers produced in late summer, this aster is quite unsurpassed. The color blends beautifully with schemes in soft tints, but is equally good for cooling down the orange and bright yellow of *Crocosmia*, *Coreopsis* and *Rudbeckia*. It is not the sort of aster that has to be kept constantly on the move to flourish— plant it in good soil in the first place and leave it alone. Good for picking.

Size H: 3 ft.; S: 1–1½ ft. **Aspect** Full sun. **Soil** Well enriched with compost or manure. **Propagation** Division in spring. **Planting partners** Make a flower bed of this aster, catmint (*Nepeta*), *Tulipa* 'White Triumphator,' *Lilium regale* and *Anemone × hybrida* (Japanese anemone).

Astrantia major
'Shaggy'
(Masterwort)

Delightful old-fashioned plant, each pale pink flower like a Victorian posy, lovely for picking, and with a long-flowering season, especially if dead-headed. In this cultivar the outer circlet of bracts is much larger than usual and tipped with green.

Size H: 2–2½ ft.; S: 1–1½ ft. **Aspect** Sun or part-shade. **Soil** Most, if not too dry. **Propagation** Division; it will self-seed but seed-lings will be variable. **Planting part-ners** *Brunnera*, *Astilbe*, *Campanula*.

Baby's breath see *Gypsophila*

Anthemis tinctoria 'E.C. Buxton'

Baptisia australis
(False indigo)

Rather like a lupin, but whereas lupins are not long-lived, once you have established *Baptisia* it is a permanent resident of the garden; what is more, you must never disturb it as it hates being moved. *Baptisia* takes time to establish and to be in full flowering form. You should not expect it to flower the first year after planting it. Graceful stems 4 ft. tall of blue-green trifoliate leaves, remaining attractive and fresh throughout the seasons, are decorated in mid-summer with spires of pea flowers in soft indigo blue. Native to eastern United States.

Size H: 4 ft.; S: 2 ft. **Aspect** Full sun. **Soil** Lime-free or neutral, not too dry. **Propagation** Seed. **Planting part-ners** *Hemerocallis lilioasphodelus*, *Paradisea liliastrum*.

Campanula lactiflora

also inclined to revert to plain green, to which 'Hadspen Cream' is not so prone.
Size H: 15 in.; S: 2 ft. **Aspect** Part- or full shade. **Soil** Fertile, not too dry. **Propagation** Division. **Planting partners** *Scilla siberica*, *Epimedium*.

Burning bush see *Dictamnus albus purpureus*

Californian tree poppy see *Romneya coulteri*

Campanula lactiflora
(Bellflower)

With upright stems and loose panicles of starry bellflowers in summer, in delicate shades of milky blue, or sometimes pink and white, this is an old trooper of the herbaceous border. Despite its height, you should get away without staking, except in windy areas. If you start off with violet-blue 'Prichard's Variety,' it will seed itself and you will end up with a lovely colony of mixed pale colors. It likes soil rich in organic matter and sun, but will grow and flower in poorer conditions. Native to the Caucasus.
Size H: 5 ft.; S: 2 ft. **Aspect** Sun or part-shade. **Soil** Any, provided drainage is good. **Propagation** Division or seed. **Planting partners** old-fashioned roses, *Phlox*, *Lilium regale*, *Alchemilla mollis*.

Clematis × durandii

This has *Clematis integrifolia*, a herbaceous species, as one of its parents. It makes a wonderful summer plant for the flower border, as its stems drape themselves over nearby plants, displaying their rich violet-blue flowers and allowing you to see them at close quarters, rather than on some distant wall.
Size H: 6 ft. (sprawler). **Aspect** Sun or part-shade. **Propagation** By division if you dare. **Pruning** Cut back to 2½ ft. in late autumn, or spring in colder areas. **Planting partners** Early bulbs planted close to it and Oriental poppies (*Papaver orientale*) nearby (the *Clematis* will grow and conceal their dying foliage).

Cranesbill see *Geranium*

Dahlia
'Bishop of Llandaff'

From late summer until frost, single glowing scarlet flowers, with centers that seem neatly embroidered with darkest crimson knot stitch, lift this plant into a class of its own—a picture of refinement with its own built-in color scheme. The metallic dark bronze-purple foliage adds to the garden scene from the moment it pushes through the soil. Good for picking.
Size H: 3 ft.; S: 2 ft. **Aspect** Sun. **Soil** Rich in organic matter. **Propagation** Division of the tuber or cuttings in spring (see page 90). **Planting partners** A key plant for hot color schemes (see pages 60–61) and also lovely with silver foliage.

Bellflower see *Campanula lactiflora*

Bleeding heart see *Dicentra spectabilis*

Brunnera macrophylla
'Hadspen Cream'

Heart-shaped leaves, very beautifully splashed in cream and bluish green, stay for most of the year on this low, mounded, easily grown herbaceous plant, suitable for the front of your shadier beds. In spring, sprays of brilliant blue forget-me-not flowers hover above the foliage to delightful effect. You may have seen *Brunnera macrophylla* 'Dawson's White,' the leaves of which are even more prettily variegated, but this latter is a much more delicate plant, its leaves scorch badly with too much wind or sun and it is

Dahlia merckii

With little mauve-pink flowers on slender stalks airily poised above a mass of finely dissected leaves, this charming species is as unlike the dinner-plate dahlias as you could imagine. Flowers for months from summer on and, if deeply planted in the first place, will not need autumn lifting, except in cold areas. Good for picking. Native to Mexico.

Size H: 3 ft.; S: 2 ft. **Aspect** Full sun. **Soil** Rich in organic matter. **Propagation** Seed or division of tuber. **Planting partners** Soft color schemes (see pages 68–9).

Daylily see *Hemerocallis lilioasphodelus*

Dicentra spectabilis

(Bleeding heart)

With pendant heart-shaped lockets in rosy-pink and white, dangling from slender arching stems above soft, fern-like fresh green leaves, this well-loved late-spring-flowering herbaceous plant deserves a place in the smallest garden. *D. spectabilis alba* is the exquisite white form. Most attractive to slugs, so you will need to lay down slug bait. Native to Siberia, Japan and China.

Size H: 2 ft.; S: 1½ ft. **Aspect** Part-shade. **Soil** Rich in organic matter, not too dry. **Propagation** Division or seed. **Planting partners** Ferns, *Smilacina*, *Hyacinthoides non-scripta* (bluebells).

Dictamnus albus purpureus

(Burning bush)

With racemes of early-summer pretty pink flowers veined in purple, handsome star-shaped seedpods, fragrant leaves when you crush them, robust stems that require no staking, this thoroughly reliable old garden plant is a long-term investment, to be put into the right place first time and then left alone as it will not stand disturbance. Known as burning bush on account of the volatile oils which it produces; these have been known to ignite on warm summer evenings. The seed pods have a delicious smell of oranges. Native to Europe and Asia.

Size H: 2–3 ft.; S: 2 ft. **Aspect** Full sun. **Soil** Well prepared at the outset (see page 81). **Propagation** Seed. **Planting partners** *Aquilegia* (pink), *Erigeron philadelphicus*.

Dierama pulcherrimum

(Angel's fishing rod, Wandflower)

As if floating on air, suspended on long arching stems of incredible grace, flower bells in mauve, rose-pink, purple and white sway and shimmer with each breath of wind in late summer. The singular habit of this beautiful South African member of the iris family requires an isolated position to display itself properly. You often see it planted beside water, where it looks appropriate, but remember the last thing it wants is waterlogged soil. The grass-like, evergreen leaves need an annual cleaning out of the old leaves in spring (use scissors, as the foliage is

surprisingly tough). Good for picking. **Size** H: 4 ft.; S: 2 ft. **Aspect** Full sun. **Soil** Warm, well drained. **Propagation** Seed or division; from the base of the corm is a brittle, long, fleshy white root—take care not to damage this when dividing. **Planting partners** Lawn, paving or water.

Digitalis grandiflora

(Yellow foxglove)

Unlike the ordinary, much-loved biennial wild foxglove (*D. purpurea*), this is perennial, with softly hairy pale yellow "gloves," netted with pale brown inside, in summer. Good for picking. Native to southern Europe.

Size H: 2 ft.; S: 1–1½ ft. **Aspect** Sun or shade. **Soil** With added organic matter. **Propagation** Seed. **Planting partner** *Hosta* 'Halcyon.'

Dierama pulcherrimum

113

Eryngium alpinum
(Sea holly)

The jewel in the crown of thistle-like plants. An incredibly fine, lacy, metallic blue ruff (that looks prickly but is quite soft to touch) surrounds the central cone of summer flower, the stems are washed in violet and the effect of the plant in bloom is one of shimmering blue. Despite its common name, it comes from high meadows in the Alps, and thus requires an open, sunny site. Good for picking. Native to central and southern Europe.

Size H: 2½ ft.; S: 2 ft. **Aspect** Full sun. **Soil** Well drained. **Propagation** Division or seed. **Planting partners** Silver-leaved plants.

Eryngium alpinum

Erysimum
'Bowles' Mauve'

An indispensable plant with a wild enthusiasm for flowering, in mild climates it produces its lilac-purple flowers almost the whole year round, nicely complemented by gray-green leaves. Best planted in dry, gravelly, limy soil in full sun, it will be longer-lived than on rich soil, where it puts on too much foliage in proportion to its small root and becomes unstable. Renew often from heel cuttings in summer, taken while the plant is still young—once it becomes old and woody the cuttings are much slower to root. Good for picking.

Size H and S: 2 ft. **Aspect** Full sun. **Soil** Poor, limy. **Propagation** Cuttings (see above). **Planting partners** *Anthemis cupaniana*, other silver-foliage plants.

Eupatorium maculatum atropurpureum
(Joe Pye weed)

As a late arrival on the garden scene in early autumn, just when a dramatic effect is most welcome, along comes this American roadside weed to steal the scene with its imposing 7 ft. purple-tinged stems, whorled leaves with reddish veins, topped with flat heads of fluffy flowers, the color of mashed blackcurrants and the size of pudding plates. Native to North America.

Size H: 7 ft.; S: 3 ft. **Aspect** Sun or part-shade. **Soil** Rich in organic matter, not too dry. **Propagation** Division. **Planting partners** *Anemone × hybrida*, *Hydrangea*, white.

Euphorbia characias wulfenii

A plant that can fit in wherever you care to place it—among shrubs, in flower borders, in gravel, on hot, dry banks, in situations both wild and formal—it seems to play whatever part you wish. A structural plant of great quality, the gray-blue linear evergreen leaves arranged in whorls around the upright stems remain decorative throughout the year, with a bonus in spring of handsome, long-lasting, brilliant lime-green heads of flower—just the plant to add form and interest to a hitherto shapeless border. Around mid-summer cut the old flowering stems to the base, to make room for the new growth (some people are allergic to the poisonous milky sap *Euphorbia* exudes). Seedlings will transplant but leave older plants alone. Native to the Balkans, European Turkey.

Size H and S: 4 ft. **Aspect** Sun. **Soil** Most, if well drained, even poor, dry soil. **Propagation** Seed. **Planting partners** *Artemisia* 'Powis Castle,' *Cistus*.

Euphorbia griffithii
'Dixter'

Young shoots push through the ground in spring, unfolding a mass of lance-shaped rich mahogany-red leaves, each with a pinkish mid-rib. Atop the rising stems the buds slowly develop, opening into clusters of flower-like bracts with the vivid tones of a blood orange. Decorative for weeks, the branching wands of foliage turn green with a bronze flush by

summer, but still act as pleasing background. Good for picking.
Size H: 3 ft.; S: 2 ft. **Aspect** Sun or part-shade. **Soil** Moist for preference, but the running root is more easily contained when the soil is not too rich. **Propagation** Division. **Planting partners** Dazzling combined with *Valeriana phu* 'Aurea,' *Euphorbia dulcis* 'Chameleon' and *Narcissus* (daffodils) in spring.

Fair maids of France see ***Ranunculus aconitifolius*** 'Flore Pleno'

False indigo see ***Baptisia australis***

Gentiana asclepiadea
(Willow gentian)

One of the few flowers belonging to autumn that are pure bright blue, the willow gentian with its graceful arching stems bedecked with azure trumpets is a valuable plant, deserving of your best position in rich, moist soil and part- or full shade. Make sure you put it in the right place first time (this plant will not tolerate transplanting) and give it room to display itself properly. Also recommended is *G. asclepiadea* 'Knightshayes' (a lighter blue, with white inside the flowers). Native to Europe and western Asia.
Size H: 1½ ft.; S: 2 ft. **Aspect** Part or full shade. **Soil** Rich, moisture-retentive. **Propagation** Seed, or cuttings when young shoots are 2–3 in. long in spring. **Planting partners** *Hosta*

(small), *Ranunculus aconitifolius* 'Flore Pleno' (which likes the same conditions and will have died back before the gentian flowers).

Geranium
'Ann Folkard'
(Cranesbill)

You could almost make a garden from the wonderful genus of *Geranium* alone, they are such adaptable, easy and useful plants, flowering from summer on. This cranesbill, a hybrid between *Geranium psilostemon* and *G. procurrens*, inherits the best characteristics from each parent—its color from the former and its trailing habit (but without invasive tendencies) from the latter. It sometimes masquerades as a climber, entwining its stems through nearby plants—you can get a sudden illusion that they, too, have vivid magenta flowers, veined in black, with velvety black middles. A super, long-flowering plant, rather scarce but worth every effort to obtain.
Size H and S: 3–4 ft., trailing. **Aspect** Sun or part-shade. **Soil** Any, provided drainage is good. **Propagation** Best left alone, but try cuttings in spring. **Planting partners** Underplant with spring bulbs. Marvelous rambling through gray foliage.

Geranium endressii
(Cranesbill)

A maid of all work, a boon to the busy gardener, this ever-obliging plant can be counted on to give of its best

anywhere in the garden—in sun or shade, in any soil you care to offer it. The legendary gardener Margery Fish said, in *An All the Year Garden*: "I have one gardening rule—when in doubt, plant *Geranium endressii*." Making a wonderful filler for new gardens, its cheerful bright pink flowers in summer and autumn and light green foliage seem just as appropriate in forgotten, shady corners as they do in the prime position of your best flower bed. After it has been blooming for several months and become rather ragged, cut it back, and after a short rest it will be back to its carefree smiling self. Native to the Pyrenees.
Size H: 1 ft.; S: 1½ ft. **Aspect** Any. **Soil** Any, except waterlogged. **Propagation** Division whenever you feel like it. **Planting partners** Looks good under pink cabbage roses, such as *Rosa* 'Constance Spry' or 'Caroline Testout.'

Gentiana asclepiadea

Geranium × *riversleaianum*
'Russell Prichard'
(Cranesbill)

This cranesbill should be in a book of records under "longest flowering season." A seemingly endless display—for five to six months—of rich pink flowers appear, beautifully complemented by the grayish-green leaves. A hybrid, one of its parents is the slightly tender *G. traversii* from the South Pacific, so choose a warm place when planting—it loves to bask over hot paving stones. Such generosity seems to wear the plant out, so frequent propagation is advisable.
Size H: 9 in.; S: 3 ft. **Aspect** Full sun. **Soil** Any, provided it is well drained. **Propagation** Divide every few years in late spring. **Planting partners** *Artemisia*, *Sedum*.

Geranium wallichianum
'Buxton's Variety'
(Cranesbill)

A very variable species, often purply-pink as shown here, 'Buxton's Variety' is the aristocrat among cranesbills. A low, trailing plant, it produces clear blue saucer-shaped flowers with large white centers, a delight in late summer and autumn when it goes on and on displaying its lovely flowers. This species comes from damp Himalayan meadows, so it likes a moister spot than most members of this genus.
Size H: 1 ft.; S: 3 ft. **Aspect** Sun or part-shade in dry gardens. **Soil** Plenty of organic matter, not too dry. **Propagation** Division or seed, seedlings may vary. **Planting partners** Underplant with *Erythronium* and other small spring bulbs, including *Tulipa sprengeri*, the last tulip to flower, which will seed happily beneath the *Geranium* foliage.

Giant cowslip see *Primula florindae*

Gillenia trifoliata

A charming native of eastern North America, a well-mannered herbaceous plant that looks presentable throughout the season. Little white flowers in summer, blushed pink on reddish stems, flutter over neat, trifoliate leaves. After petal-fall, the plant remains quietly pretty, as the soft red calyces linger on at the end of summer. Just before it retires below ground for winter, the leaves go out in a flash of brilliant scarlet. Good for picking. Native to United States and Canada.
Size H: 3 ft.; S: 2 ft. **Aspect** Any. **Soil** Neutral or acid. **Propagation** Seed or division (needs no regular division). **Planting partners** *Hosta sieboldiana* var. *elegans*.

Gypsophila
'Rosenschleier'
('Veil of Roses,' 'Rosy Veil')
(Baby's breath)

A billowing mass of tiny, very pale pink double flowers in summer, light as thistle down, and lovely for picking, envelop low mounds of blue-gray foliage. Ideal for the front of a sunny border, unlike some *Gypsophila*, this one is long-lived when grown in well-drained soil in full sun. Do not disturb once planted, and cut it back immediately after flowering to encourage a second flush in autumn.
Size H: 1 ft.; S: 2 ft. **Aspect** Full Sun. **Soil** Well drained; likes lime. **Propagation** Cuttings. **Planting partners** *Nerine*, silver-foliage plants, early bulbs that will have time to complete their life-cycle before the *Gypsophila* gets going.

Kniphofia 'Little Maid'

Hemerocallis lilioasphodelus
(Daylily)

An easy, trouble-free, robust plant, the sort you can forget all about, until you notice what seems to be an early-flowering lily, with lemon-yellow trumpet flowers in late spring, tips curved back to the petals, arising from a fountain of mid-green leaves. When you realize this lovely thing is also very fragrant, and is happily flowering away with no attention at all, you can understand why it has been a favorite garden plant for centuries. Good for picking. Native to eastern Asia.

Size H: 2½ ft.; S: 1½ ft. **Aspect** Sun or part-shade. **Soil** Not too dry, apply general fertilizer in spring. **Propagation** Division every few years. **Planting partners** *Lupinus* (lupins), *Stachys macrantha superba, Paradisea liliastrum*.

Himalayan blue poppy see *Meconopsis × sheldonii*

Horned violet see *Viola cornuta*

Iris pallida pallida
syn. *Iris pallida dalmatica*

A bearded iris with translucent lavender-blue scented flowers, and lovely gray-blue spiky fans of leaves. Usually, after bearded irises have flowered in early summer, all you have for the remainder of the season is foliage that gradually deteriorates into a mess. But the leaves of *I. pallida* *pallida* remain fresh right through to autumn, forming a useful upright contrast with low surrounding plants. 'Argentea Variegata' and 'Variegata' (striped in white and pale yellow, respectively) are less tall, both are very decorative, and fairly slow to increase. Good for picking. Native to western Yugoslavia.

Size H: 3 ft.; S: 1 ft. **Aspect** Full sun. **Soil** Rich, well drained, preferably slightly limy. **Propagation** Division of rhizomes in late summer, every three years. **Planting partners** *Weigela praecox* 'Variegata' and a carpet of *Lamium maculatum* 'Beacon Silver.'

Japanese anemone see *Anemone × hybrida*

Joe Pye weed see *Eupatorium maculatum atropurpureum*

Knautia macedonica

Flowers like little crimson pincushions appear for months on end from summer to autumn. Seems to fit into many different color schemes, flops about a little, but is such a charming plant that it is no trouble to surround it with a low metal hoop (see page 98). Good for picking. Native to central Europe.

Size H: 2½ ft.; S: 2 ft. **Aspect** Full sun. **Soil** Well drained. **Propagation** Basal cuttings in spring. **Planting partners** *Hosta fortunei* 'Albomarginata' or some other plant with good white variegation.

Kniphofia
'Little Maid'
(Red-hot poker)

For all those who think of red-hot pokers as the most vulgar plants imaginable, this is one of the prettiest plants for the late-summer garden. Bred by Beth Chatto, this small poker is a dear little plant, with pale creamy-yellow spikes of flower in late summer and neat, grassy foliage. Native to South Africa, *Kniphofia* are plants for the first-class spots only; it is no use trying to grow them unless you can provide them with plenty of sun, moisture in summer, good drainage at all times and a very fertile soil. Good for picking.

Size H: 2 ft.; S: 15 in. **Aspect** Full sun. **Soil** Fertile, well drained. **Propagation** Division in spring, but unless you need more, leave undisturbed. **Planting partners** *Aster thomsonii* 'Nanus,' small blue *Agapanthus*.

Geranium wallichianum

Lobelia 'Queen Victoria'

Lady's mantle see *Alchemilla mollis*

Lobelia
'Queen Victoria'

With spires of glowing scarlet flowers and lustrous dark purple foliage, this herbaceous lobelia is a striking addition to the late-summer border. Once you have built up a stock, grow a few on in pots and use them to fill late-summer gaps—it does not mind being moved even when nearly in bloom. In late spring, when you are quite sure the soil has warmed up, divide each plant into single rosettes, replenish the soil with compost or well-rotted manure, and replant.

Size H: 3 ft.; S: 1 ft. **Aspect** Sun or part-shade. **Soil** Rich in organic matter and moisture-retentive. **Propagation** Division or autumn cuttings—1–1½ in. pieces of the flower stem, with a leaf on top, firmly sunk in a pot filled with cuttings compost (see page 92), leaving the leaf sitting on the surface, and over-wintered under glass. **Planting partners** Wonderful in hot color schemes with *Dahlia* 'Bishop of Llandaff' and *Verbena* 'Lawrence Johnston.'

Loosestrife see *Lysimachia ephemerum*

Lysimachia ephemerum
(Loosestrife)

A very refined loosestrife—the epitome of subtle, cool coloring—with slender spires of small, palest gray flowers in summer and glaucous blue-gray leaves. Unlike other, more invasive, members of the genus, it stays tidily precisely where you put it. Good for picking. Native to southwestern Europe.

Size H: 3 ft.; S: 1 ft. **Aspect** Sun or part-shade. **Soil** Rich in organic matter and moisture-retentive. **Propagation** Division. **Planting partner** *Anaphalis triplinervis.*

Macleaya cordata
(Plume poppy)

Very beautiful, large, shapely, deeply lobed leaves, blue-gray above and gray-white beneath, on tall stems powdered with whitish bloom, topped by airy panicles of dainty creamy flowers in summer, this is a plant with such a strong, architectural presence that it deserves placement in a position where it can properly display itself by keeping the surrounding planting low. It does spread, but nothing like as invasively as does its first cousin, *M. microcarpa*. (Most plants labeled *M. cordata* in the nursery trade are not in fact the true plant.) Good for picking. Native to China and Japan.

Size H: 7 ft.; S: 2 ft. **Aspect** Sun or part-shade. **Soil** Any, provided drainage is good. **Propagation** Division. **Planting partners** Lovely with soft colors but also superb with hot color schemes (see pages 60–61). Interplant with early bulbs.

Malva moschata alba
(Musk mallow)

This lovely form of musk mallow, with pure white flowers in summer and dark green divided leaves, is an easy, self-perpetuating plant that looks after itself. Although perennial, it is not long-lived and as soon as plants get old and woody, pull them out and let the young ones take over. Good for picking. Native to Europe and northwestern Africa.

Size H: 2½ ft.; S: 2 ft. **Aspect** Sun or part-shade. **Soil** Well drained. **Propagation** Seed. **Planting partners** Try using it planted repetitively down the front of a border.

Masterwort see *Astrantia major*

Meadow rue see *Thalictrum delavayi*

Meconopsis × *sheldonii*
'Slieve Donard'
(Himalayan blue poppy)

A superb Himalayan poppy, with shimmering, brilliant blue nodding flowers in early summer, held on straight stems above rosettes of oblong, shallow-toothed pale green leaves with reddish brown hairs. Worth every effort to please, this beautiful plant needs cool, moist conditions—the nearest you can get to a Himalayan mist, where plants are almost permanently saturated in droplets of moisture.
Size H: 4 ft.; S: 1½ ft. **Aspect** Part-shade. **Soil** Rich in organic matter, lime-free or neutral, moist but well drained. **Propagation** Division every three years, in autumn or spring, or the plants will deteriorate; work in well-rotted manure before replanting. **Planting partners** *Astilbe*, *Rodgersia*.

Morina longifolia
(Whorlflower)

This plant is also from the Himalayas but much more adaptable than *Meconopsis*. It is a very distinguished thistle-like plant, with prickly foliage and stems decorated with sharp whorls of little white tubular flowers in summer, which blush with pink after they have been pollinated. Its tidy presentation

and singular shape provide interest long after the flowers have fallen. Good seed heads for drying.
Size H: 2½ ft.; S: 15 in. **Aspect** Sun. **Soil** Well drained. **Propagation** Seed. **Planting partners** Low, carpeting plants to show off its shapely habit.

Musk mallow see *Malva moschata alba*

Nectaroscordum siculum

This plant (formerly listed under *Allium* so one thinks of it in the same bracket) has umbels of strangely pretty dangling green bells, washed with purple. In the wild it grows in damp, shady woods so you can use it to add height to cooler borders in early summer. It seems such an unusual plant, at first sight, that you cannot believe there will ever be too much of it. But there comes a time when you want to call a stop and pick the seed heads before they drop their seed. Good for picking; good seed heads for drying. Native to France and Italy.
Size H: 3 ft.; S: 1 ft. **Aspect** Sun or part-shade. **Soil** Any, provided drainage is good. **Propagation** Division or seed. **Planting partners** *Lamium maculatum* 'Beacon Silver,' *Viola cornuta*.

Nerine undulata

One of the joys of mid-autumn, just when there seems nothing else to look forward to, is this little bulb, with

umbels of frilly flowers in tender pink, each petal delicately crinkled along the edges, and narrow, strap-shaped wintergreen leaves. In the cool, late-season weather, the flowers last for weeks. Much coveted by garden visitors, this delightful little plant should not be given away too freely as you will want your clump to increase. Deserving of the warmest spot in a garden, preferably under a sunny wall. Good for picking. Native to South Africa.
Size H: 15 in.; S: 8 in. **Aspect** Full sun, sheltered position. **Soil** Light, well drained, plus well-rotted compost and bonemeal for initial planting. **Propagation** Division every three to four years. **Planting partner** *Iris unguicularis*.

Morina longifolia

Paeonia mlokosewitschii
(Peony)

An enthralling plant in spring, as the plump shining dark red shoots emerge from the soil, slowly swell and expand into downy, dusky purple, crimson-veiled leaves. By flowering time, in late spring, the foliage has turned to soft bluish green, a fitting background for the large, single blooms, in clear lemon. You might say that this peony is rather fleeting of flower, but you could also argue that when in bloom it is indeed the goddess of the garden. Good for picking if you can bear to. Native to eastern-central Caucasus.
Size H: 2½ ft.; S: 2 ft. **Aspect** Full sun. **Soil** Well drained, enriched with well-rotted manure or compost, plus bonemeal; be careful to plant at the same level as it was in the pot, and when mulching in spring, do not smother the crowns. **Propagation** Division in early autumn; seed. **Planting partners** *Aquilegia*, blue, *Brunnera macrophylla*.

*Paeonia
mlokosewitschii*

Papaver orientale
hybrids

Huge flamboyant poppies, with glistening, crumpled-silk petals, blotched at the base with darkest maroon, their radiant colors and extravagant size lending dazzle and excitement to the early-summer border. Choose 'Goliath' in dashing scarlet, 'Turkish Delight' in salmon, 'May Queen' with double, vivid orange flowers—if you like your colors hot and strong. And there is 'Black and White' or 'Cedric's Pink' (a ravishing soft, dusky pink) for those with quieter taste. The rough mid-green leaves of these poppies die away soon after they have flowered.
Size H: 2–4 ft.; S: 2–3 ft. **Aspect** Full sun. **Soil** Rich in organic matter, well drained. **Propagation** Division or root cuttings (if you move them they will regenerate from bits of root left behind). **Planting partners** *Clematis × durandii* or *Lathyrus latifolius* 'Albus,' planted nearby, to hide the gap when the poppies' foliage has died down.

Pasque flower see *Pulsatilla vulgaris*

Pearl everlasting see *Anaphalis triplinervis*

Penstemon
'Evelyn'

Penstemons have a reputation for being slightly tender and short-lived but 'Evelyn' is a reliable, neat little plant, hardier than most, with a summer-long supply of pretty pink flowers with pale striped throats and tidy linear leaves, a little topper of a plant for the small garden. All penstemons look rather tatty by the end of the winter and should be pruned and tidied in spring. Do not be tempted to do this too soon—you will encourage them to put on new growth only to have it blasted by late frost.
Size H and S: 1½ ft. **Aspect** Full sun. **Soil** Rich in organic matter, well drained. **Propagation** Cuttings. **Planting partners** *Dianthus* (pinks), *Artemisia canescens*, *Geranium sanguineum striatum*.

Perovskia
'Blue Spire'
(Russian sage)

An excellent sub-shrub with aromatic leaves, deserving of your hottest, sunniest spot. Inclining itself gracefully toward the sun, it stays in bloom for many weeks in late summer. Luminous pale gray stems, with toothed, gray-green leaves smelling of rosemary when crushed, branch into elegant spires holding whorls of lavender-blue velveteen bobbles. Prune it hard back in spring to keep it compact.

Size H: 4 ft.; S: 2 ft. **Aspect** Full sun. **Soil** Well drained, with added grit. **Propagation** Cuttings. **Planting partners** Gray foliage, *Calamintha nepeta*, *Lavandula* (lavender).

Pimpinella major
'Rosea'

A pretty plant, like a pink cow parsley or Queen Anne's lace, with finely cut ferny foliage and umbels of little pale rose flowers in summer. Delightful, not particularly easy to obtain, but worth the effort. Good for picking. Native to Europe.

Size H: 2 ft.; S: 1 ft. **Aspect** Sun or part-shade. **Soil** Any, provided drainage is good. **Propagation** Division. **Planting partner** *Iris pallida* 'Argentea Variegata.'

Plume poppy see *Macleaya cordata*

Primula florindae
(Giant cowslip)

Flowering later than most primulas, in mid-summer and beyond, this handsome, robust plant is especially valuable as, although its favorite habitat is rich, moist soil by the waterside, it will still grow happily, flower and seed itself around in an ordinary border, even if the soil is on the dry side. Fragrant, pendant, sulfur-yellow bell-shaped flowers, powdered with farina, top slender stems arising from clumps of rounded leaves. Native to Tibet.

Size H: 2 ft.; S: 1 ft. **Aspect** Sun or part-shade. **Soil** See above. **Propagation** Seed. **Planting partners** *Hosta* 'Halcyon,' *Viola* (purple).

Pulsatilla vulgaris
(Pasque flower)

The flower, stems and emerging leaves of the pasque flower, one of the most beautiful plants of spring, are clothed in gossamer-fine silky, silvery hairs. The bell-shaped flowers, with glistening petals, are usually mauve or violet, but you can also find pasque flowers in soft red, pink, white and even pure blue. Ideal plant for the front of a sunny border. Native to Europe.

Size H and S: 1 ft. **Aspect** Full sun. **Soil** Well drained, preferably limy. **Propagation** Seed. **Planting partners** *Primula auricula* 'Old Irish Blue.'

Ranunculus aconitifolius
'Flore Pleno'
(Fair maids of France)

A lovely, old-fashioned plant with little pure-white button flowers, double and very neat, born on branching stems with dark green, deeply divided leaves—a beautiful antique plant to be carefully tended in rich, moist soil. Good for picking.

Size H: 2 ft.; S: 1½ ft. **Aspect** Sun or part-shade. **Soil** Rich in organic matter and moisture-retentive. **Propagation** Division. **Planting partners** *Gentiana asclepiadea*, *Codonopsis clematidea* to fill in the gap later on.

Red-hot poker see *Kniphofia*

Penstemon 'Evelyn'

Rodgersia pinnata
'Superba'

Handsome leaves—deeply veined, stiff, crinkled and rough to touch —burnished dark bronzy red and shaped rather like those of a horse chestnut, remain highly picturesque throughout the growing season, a superb contrast in texture with its feathery plumes of bright pink flowers in summer. With their telling clumps of bold foliage, *Rodgersia* make a dramatic impact. They play an important part in the orchestra of leaves—use them for inventing garden pictures out of foliage alone. Good for picking.

Size H and S: 3 ft. **Aspect** Sun, or part-shade in hot gardens. **Soil** Rich in organic matter and moisture-retentive; will thrive in bog gardens. **Propagation** Division. **Planting partners** *Hosta*, *Euphorbia griffithii* 'Dixter.'

Romneya coulteri

appear in summer and autumn, when picked, last in water. Once established, it is a very invasive plant, but who would care? Prune in spring to within 1 ft. of the base. Very intolerant of root disturbance. Native to California.

Size H: 6 ft.; S: 4 ft. **Aspect** Full sun in a warm, sheltered position. **Soil** Light, well drained. **Propagation** Not easy but try cuttings from the base in spring, root cuttings in winter, or seed. **Planting partners** Silver-leaved plants such as *Artemisia ludoviciana*, *Crinum × powellii* 'Album.'

Roscoea cautleoides

This choice small plant, a member of the ginger family, with lovely clear lemon flowers in summer, somewhat like orchids, arising from sheaves of shining green leaves, has all the appearance of being difficult. But in fact it is an easy, long-lived plant, although it does not appear above ground until nigh on mid-summer. Deserves a nice spot in the front of the border, carefully marked with canes, so you do not dig it up by mistake. The Kew form of *Roscoea cautleoides* is even better if you can get hold of it— a more compact plant, with larger flowers. Native to China.

Size H: 15 in.; S: 6 in. **Aspect** Part-shade. **Soil** Moist, plenty of humus. **Propagation** Division in spring or seed. **Planting partners** Interplant with early-flowering bulbs.

Salvia × superba
syn. *S. nemorosa* 'Superba'

Salvia are mostly tender but this is a thoroughly reliable, good garden plant with upright, rather woody stems, aromatic foliage, and branching slender spikes of violet-blue flowers in summer with reddish purple bracts and stems. Good for picking.

Size H: 3 ft.; S: 1½ ft. **Aspect** Full sun. **Soil** Fertile, well drained. **Propagation** Division, or basal cuttings in spring. **Planting partners** Lovely with pale yellow, such as *Anthemis tinctoria* 'E.C. Buxton' and *Rosa* 'Graham Thomas.'

Sea holly see *Eryngium alpinum*

Sedum
'Herbstfreude' syn. *S.* 'Autumn Joy'

Neat rosettes of pale sea-green fleshy leaves are a soothing background color all summer. In late summer the wide, flat heads of sea-green buds slowly suffuse with pink until they are rich rosy salmon, and have become a landing pad for butterflies sipping nectar from the flowers. As autumn progresses the flowers fade gradually to rich brown and keep their shape throughout winter. Common it may be, but this is a thoroughly useful plant that contributes to the garden scene throughout the year. Good for picking and drying.

Size H and S: 2 ft. **Aspect** Full sun.

Romneya coulteri
(Californian tree poppy)

A plant you will find in books on shrubs, where the author will insist it is a shrub, but also in books on herbaceous plants—once seen you will understand why people would want to fight over it. You might have to make several attempts to establish the Californian tree poppy, before it will finally get the message and start growing. When it finally unwraps its first, exquisitely beautiful large satiny-white saucer-shaped flower, the crinkled silk petals surrounding an aureole of golden stamens, you will sink your nose therein to discover that this lovely thing has a fragrance that seems to change from ripe apricots to old-fashioned laundry soap. The foliage is blue-gray, and the flowers, which

Soil Well drained. **Propagation** Division or cuttings. **Planting partners** *Artemisia*, *Nerine*, *Verbena*.

Selinum tenuifolium

An architectural plant, like a stately cow parsley, bringing a breath of spring into dusty late summer, with its beautiful fern-like leaves forming a filigree of fresh green, and umbels of tiny, cool creamy-white flowers. Good for picking. Native to Himalayas (India and western Pakistan).
Size H: 4 ft.; S: 2 ft. **Aspect** Sun or part-shade, not too hot a position. **Soil** Any provided drainage is good. **Propagation** Seed or division, by very carefully chopping a small piece off (it does not like being disturbed). **Planting partners** Low-growing plants, to set off its elegant shape.

Thalictrum delavayi
(Meadow rue)

Tall, elegant and ravishingly pretty, once you have one plant, you will immediately want to make a large group. Panicles of tiny, rich lilac flowers in mid- to late summer, each a perfect miniature, held by stems so fine they seem suspended on air, form a mist of mauve blossom. Neat little mid-green leaves complete the picture. Good for picking. Native to western China.
Size H: 5 ft.; S: 2 ft. **Aspect** Sun or part-shade. **Soil** Preferably rich in organic matter and moisture-retentive. **Propagation** Division or seed.

Planting partners *Anaphalis triplinervis, Viola cornuta*.

Verbena bonariensis

Self-propagating and self-supporting, long-flowering and indifferent to hot, dry conditions, this excellent late-summer plant is as good to look at as it is useful. Tall, slender stems support tight little clusters of lilac-purple flowers, and as summer progresses the stems branch and rebranch, flowering at every tip, eventually forming a filmy haze of mauve. Not a particularly long-lived plant, but there usually seem to be young plants ready to take over. Good for picking. Native to South America.
Size H: 4–5 ft.; S: 2 ft. **Aspect** Sun. **Soil** Well drained, light. **Propagation** Seed; will self-sow. **Planting partners** Silver foliage.

Viola cornuta
(Horned violet)

The horned violet, so called because of the slender spur or "horn" at the back of the flower, is a true perennial, unlike some violas that need regular propagation. *V. cornuta* itself has violet flowers, but forms may also be found in lilac and white. Damp summers are much to its liking, when it will flower over a long period in a cool, moist position. A ruthless cutting back after mid-summer will encourage tuffets of fresh foliage and more flowers. Use in the front of shady borders, among ferns and as ground cover under

shrubs. Native to the Pyrenees.
Size H: 6–12 in.; S: 15 in. **Aspect** Sun or part-shade. **Soil** Rich in organic matter, not too dry. **Propagation** Seed or division; change the growing position occasionally, as violas do not like growing in the same spot indefinitely. **Planting partners** *Lamium* 'Beacon Silver,' low-growing *Campanula*.

Wandflower see *Dierama pulcherrimum*

Whorlflower see *Morina longiflora*

Willow gentian see *Gentiana asclepiadea*

Viola cornuta

Index

Plant hardiness zones

This hardiness map will help you to establish which plants are most suitable for your garden. The zones 1–11 are based on the average annual minimum temperature for each zone and appear after the plant entry in the index. The lower number indicates the northernmost zone in which the plant can survive the winter and the higher number the most southerly area in which it will perform consistently.

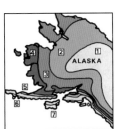

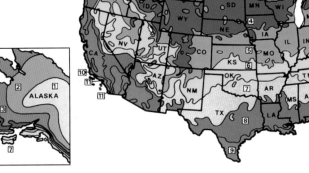

Acknowledgments

Author's acknowledgments

For their great help with this book, special thanks to my husband, Val Dillon, and also to Diane Tomlinson, Mary Rowe, Charles Nelson, Mary Davies, Jim Reynolds, Kitty Reardon, Rosemary Brown and Carole McGlynn. I owe much to the gardening wisdom gathered over many years from my two great mentors, Graham Stuart Thomas and the late David Shackleton.

Publisher's acknowledgments

The publisher thanks the following photographers and organizations for their kind permission to reproduce the photographs in this book:

1 Clay Perry/Garden Picture Library; 2–3 Georges Lévêque; 4–5 Jerry Harpur (The Old Rectory, Burghfield); 6–7 Georges Lévêque; 8 left D.Tomlinson; 8 right Georges Lévêque; 9 Clive Nichols; 10 Andrew Lawson; 11 Georges Lévêque; 12–13 Marijke Heuff (Ineke Greve, Holland); 14 Andrew Lawson; 15 Carol Hellman/Garden Picture Library; 16 Clive Nichols; 17 Pat Brindley; 20 Clive Nichols; 21 Marijke Heuff (Mr & Mrs Lauxterman, Holland); 22 Photos Horticultural; 23 Christine Ternynck; 24 D.Tomlinson; 25 Clive Nichols; 26 S & O Mathews; 27 Philippe Perdereau; 31 Georges Lévêque; 33 Jerry Harpur; 35 D.Tomlinson; 36 Brian Carter/Garden Picture Library; 37 Marianne Majerus; 40 S & O Mathews; 41 Philippe Perdereau; 42 left Jerry Harpur/Elizabeth Whiting and Associates; 42 right Clive Nichols; 43 Jerry Harpur (Park Farm, Chelmsford); 44–5 Clive Nichols; 46 Georges Lévêque; 47 Tania Midgley; 48 Jerry Pavia/Garden Picture Library; 49 Noel Kavanagh; 50 Andrew Lawson; 51 D.Tomlinson; 52 Andrew Lawson; 54 Jerry Harpur (Sticky Wicket, Buckland Newton); 55 Elizabeth Whiting and Associates; 56–7 Clive Nichols; 58 D.Tomlinson; 59 Andrew Lawson; 62 Georges Lévêque; 63 J.S. Sira/Garden Picture Library; 64 above Jacqui Hurst/Boys Syndication; 64 below Andrew Lawson; 65 S & O Mathews; 66 above Georges Lévêque; 66 below Andrew Lawson 67 Photos Horticultural; 70 Andrew Lawson; 71 Clive Nichols; 72 S & O Mathews; 73–4 Clive Nichols; 75 Garden Picture Library; 78–9 Georges Lévêque; 80 Steven Wooster/Garden Picture Library; 81 Marijke Heuff (Mr & Mrs Lauxterman, Holland); 83 D.Tomlinson; 85 Andrew Lawson; 86 Jerry Harpur (Sir Charles and Lady Fraser); 91 Georges Lévêque; 98 Jerry Harpur; 99 S & O Mathews; 100–1 Georges Lévêque; 102 D.Tomlinson; 103 John Miller; 104 John Glover/Garden Picture Library; 105–6 Clive Nichols; 107–110 Andrew Lawson; 112 D.Tomlinson; 113 Andrew Lawson; 114 D.Tomlinson; 115 Photos Horticultural; 116 Andrew Lawson; 118 Eric Crichton; 119–20 Andrew Lawson; 122 D.Tomlinson; 123 Clive Nichols/Garden Picture Library.

The publisher also thanks: Vanessa Courtier, Lesley Craig, Barbara Nash and Janet Smy, Alistair Plumb, Helen Ridge and Michael Shoebridge.